Anonymous

Flower City Cook Book

Anonymous

Flower City Cook Book

ISBN/EAN: 9783744781244

Printed in Europe, USA, Canada, Australia, Japan

Cover: Foto ©Lupo / pixelio.de

More available books at **www.hansebooks.com**

FLOWER CITY

COOK BOOK.

"*Let good digestion wait on appetite
And health on both.*"

PUBLISHED BY

THE LADIES OF THE LAKE AVENUE MEMORIAL BAPTIST CHURCH.

PRICE, 50 CENTS.

ROCHESTER, N. Y.:
POST-EXPRESS PRINTING COMPANY.
1891.

FLOWER CITY COOK BOOK.

SOUPS.

For making soup stock, a porcelain lined, or granite ware kettle with close cover is best. Into this stock kettle all pieces of meat, bones and trimmings, both cooked and uncooked may be put, and a supply of stock kept on hand at all times, for use in the making of soups and sauces.

After cooking, stock should always be cooled rapidly, as it sours if left in a warm place. If perfectly clear soup is desired, ordinary stock may be clarified by adding the whites of eggs, boiling, and then straining.

SPLIT PEA SOUP.

One pint of split peas ; one quart of boiling water; one quart of soup stock; one teaspoonful onion juice; salt and pepper.

Soak the peas over night in cold water, drain, add the boiling water, and boil until soft—about two hours,—add stock, press through the colander, return to the soup kettle, add onion juice, salt, pepper, boil up once and serve with croûtons.

MISS LELIA BARRETT.

TOMATO SOUP.

One pint canned tomatoes; one quart milk; two tablespoonfuls of flour; half teaspoonful of soda; one small onion sliced; one tablespoonful of butter; salt, red pepper.

Stew the tomatoes with the onion, rub through a coarse sieve, return to kettle and bring to a boil. Scald the milk, add butter and flour. When ready to serve add soda to the tomatoes, pour

---

☞ *Use SMITH'S COMMON SENSE Baking Powder and True-Fruit Flavoring Extracts. They are the best. See page 5.*

into the heated milk, and serve immediately. If fresh tomatoes are used take one quart and boil down to a pint. This will serve six.

MRS. W. A. MONTGOMERY.

CELERY SOUP.

Boil the root and outer pieces of celery until tender, then press through a colander. Boil one quart of milk with one slice of onion in farina kettle, add celery, a bit of butter, salt, and two tablespoonfuls of flour; serve with croûtons. Cold corn, asparagus and green peas may be used in the same way.

MRS. BIGELOW.

CLAM SOUP.

Drain the liquor from twenty-five clams and boil, skim off all scum, add the clams chopped fine, and one cup of water; *simmer* for five minutes, then add butter, salt, pepper, and one pint of milk. Remove from the fire as soon as heated.

MRS. BIGELOW.

CHICKEN SOUP.

Boil the bones and skin of a cold roast chicken slowly until the bones are dry; strain and set away to cool. When cold skin off all fat and use the stock as the basis for one of the following soups. The addition of milk, butter and one cup of cold mashed potatoes makes a good white soup. A cup of canned tomatoes makes a clear soup. Any vegetable may be used.

CROÛTONS.

Croûtons for serving with soup are made by buttering slices of bread, cutting into half-inch squares, and browning them delicately in a moderate oven. These are sprinkled on the soup just before serving.

TOMATO SOUP.

Simmer together twenty minutes one quart of canned tomatoes, one pint of stock or water, one half tablespoonful of sugar, one teaspoonful of salt and a dash of cayenne pepper. Fry one tablespoonful each of chopped onion and parsley in

---

☞ *Use SMITH'S COMMON SENSE Baking Powder and True-Fruit Flavoring Extracts. They are the best. See page 5.*

one tablespoonful of butter until yellow, add one tablespoonful of corn starch, or two of flour; stir until smooth. Strain the tomatoes, return to the kettle, add the onions, parsley, etc.; let boil once and serve with croûtons.

BOSTON COOKING SCHOOL.

FISH.

CLAM CHOWDER.

One dozen clams chopped fine, and the liquor saved; eight medium sized potatoes and three small onions sliced thin; one-half pound butter crackers; one-half pound solid salt pork; cut the pork in small slices, sprinkle over the bottom of the kettle, and fry a light brown. Add a layer of potatoes and onions; season; a layer of clams and crackers and so on. Cover with boiling water and cook slowly two hours. When ready to serve, add one half-pint of milk; bring to a boil; serve hot.

MRS. NODYNE.

FRIED OYSTERS.

For twenty-five large oysters take one cup of fine bread or cracker crumbs, a teaspoonful of salt and one of baking powder. Mix the crumbs, salt, and baking powder thoroughly; dip the oysters in egg, then into the crumbs. Have ready a kettle of very hot lard; fry the oysters a delicate brown; drain and serve.

MRS. A. J. BARRETT.

ESCALOPED OYSTERS.

Use a *shallow*, broad dish for escaloped oysters; a bright tin pie plate is excellent, as the oysters cook quickly and evenly. Put a layer of coarsely crumbed crackers and bits of butter on the bottom of the tin; cover thickly with oysters, then another layer of crumbs, and if the depth of tin allows it, another layer each of oysters and crumbs. Moisten *thoroughly* with cream or milk; dot with pieces of butter, and bake in a quick oven.

ELISE KURFUST.

☞ *Use SMITH'S COMMON SENSE Baking Powder and True-Fruit Flavoring Extracts. They are the best. See page 5.*

OYSTER FRICASSEE.

Bring twenty-five oysters to a boil in their own liquor; drain. To one coffee cup of boiling milk, thickened with one large tablespoonful of flour, add the oysters, a half-cup of the liquor, a piece of butter, a dash of cayenne; let just come to a boil. As it is taken from the fire, add the beaten yolks of two eggs and a teaspoonful of chopped parsley.

MRS. BIGELOW.

PANNED OYSTERS.

Have a spider piping hot; wash and drain your oysters; throw into the spider, stirring them constantly to prevent sticking. When the edges curl, add butter, pepper and salt; serve in a hot dish immediately. These are delicious.

MRS. M. E. W. ROOT.

STEAMED OYSTERS.

Place one quart of oysters in a granite basin, and set in a steamer. Steam until the edges curl, season with butter, salt and pepper, and pour over buttered toast. A Welch rarebit may be combined with this by pouring melted cheese on the oysters, or on the toast, and the oysters added last.

MRS. WILLIS UPTON.

OYSTERS ON TOAST.

To one quart of oysters use one cup of butter and one cup of cream or milk. Put the oysters without their liquor into the melted butter and bring to boiling point; have the cream already heated separately, turn over the oysters, let boil up; pour over thin slices of toast arranged on a platter. Serve hot.

MRS. M. C. MACK.

CREAMED OYSTERS.

Drain off the liquor from one quart of oysters, and put it on the stove to heat. Skim it, and add a small piece of butter, a cup of cream, and pepper to taste. When it comes to a boil, put in the oysters, and cook them until the edges begin to curl. Stir in a tablespoonful of flour which has been mixed smooth

---

Use SMITH'S COMMON SENSE Baking Powder and True-Fruit Flavoring Extracts. They are the best. See page 5.

with a little milk; salt. Have ready slices of toast, pour the creamed oysters over them, and serve immediately.

Miss Hattie Skinner.

FISH TURBOT.

Take a fresh white fish, steam until tender—any cold boiled or baked fish may be used,—remove the bones, separate into flakes. For the dressing, heat one pint of milk, thicken with one cup of flour and one-half cup of butter beaten to a cream; when cool add two well-beaten eggs. Fill the baking dish with alternate layers of fish and sauce; cover with bread crumbs; bake one half hour.

Mrs. A. Stevens.

CODFISH BALLS.

One cupful picked salt-codfish; two tablespoonfuls of milk; one cupful mashed potatoes; one tablespoonful of butter.

Scald the codfish and mince very fine; heat the potatoes in the milk and butter and whip in one well-beaten egg. Add the codfish while the potato is still hot; beat thoroughly; form into balls; dip in egg, then in fine crumbs; fry in very hot lard until a light brown.

Mrs. W. A. Montgomery.

A root of parsley will thrive in a flower pot set in the kitchen window, and will furnish all the parsley needed for garnishing and flavoring at an outlay of five cents.

TARTARE SAUCE FOR FISH.

One cup of butter; juice of one lemon; yolks of four eggs; pinch of cayenne pepper; one-half cup of boiling water; one teaspoonful of salt. Beat the butter to a cream; add the yolks little by little, lemon juice, pepper and salt. Cook over boiling water and beat with an egg beater while cooking, until it begins to thicken, then add the boiling water, beating all the time. Very nice for baked or boiled fish.

Mrs. Frank Upton.

☞ *Use SMITH'S COMMON SENSE Baking Powder and True-Fruit Flavoring Extracts. They are the best. See page 5.*

EGGS.

POACHED EGGS.

Drop perfectly fresh eggs into boiling water, and set back immediately where the water will not boil. Let stand until the white is jellied. Eggs are much more delicious if poached without boiling, the white then cooks without becoming leathery. Serve on slices of buttered toast. M.

EGGS POACHED IN MILK.

Cover the bottom of a saucepan to the depth of one inch with milk. When scalding hot, break into it one-half dozen eggs and poach. When the eggs are set, remove them carefully, season the milk and pour over them. Serve either on buttered toast or plain.

Mrs. H. C. Williams.

BAKED EGGS.

Grease a pie tin thoroughly, spread thickly with bread or cracker crumbs, break the eggs over them in a circle, add pepper and salt. Set in the oven to bake, until the whites are set; then slip the whole from the tin to a hot platter and serve.

Mrs. C. E. Crouch.

STUFFED EGGS.

Boil a half dozen eggs half an hour. Remove the shells, and cut in halfs lengthwise. Take the yolks and with a silver fork, rub them to a smooth paste with one tablespoonful of French mustard, one of vinegar, one of butter or olive oil, and a pinch of salt. Fill the whites with this mixture and serve each half on a crisp lettuce leaf. Some add to the yolks a tablespoonful of minced ham. If the eggs are to be prepared for a picnic, press the two halves of the egg together and twist each in a square of oiled paper, such as is used for caramels.

Mrs. Miller.

☞ *Use SMITH'S COMMON SENSE Baking Powder and True-Fruit Flavoring Extracts. They are the best. See page 5.*

STEAMED EGGS.

Break a half dozen eggs into egg cups, set them in a steamer, cover, and steam eight to ten minutes.

OYSTER OMELET.

Drain and chop fine one dozen oysters, leaving out the hard part. Beat the yolks of four eggs, add two tablespoonfuls of cream, then the chopped oysters and a pinch of salt, last the whites beaten stiff. Turn into a hot buttered saucepan; when set, put in the oven a few minutes to brown on top, slide out into a hot platter, and serve at once.

EGG OMELET, HOT.

Boil one dozen eggs four minutes, remove the shells and lightly hash; place in a bowl and turn over the following dressing: Two hard boiled eggs; one-half teaspoonful each of mustard, salt and sugar, dash of pepper, a half teacupful of boiling vinegar, and four teaspoonfuls of olive oil.

Mrs. Desmond.

OMELET.

Beat the yolks of three eggs; add a half cup of milk, and a scant half cup of bread crumbs, with a dash of pepper and a pinch of salt; let it stand ten minutes. Beat the whites of the eggs *very, very* stiff, and stir in lightly. Pour the mixture into a hot saucepan, well buttered, and stand on the stove until it begins to set; then place in a hot oven for a few moments to brown, and slip gently from the saucepan to a hot platter. Unless one has a saucepan with sloping sides, it is easier to cook the omelet entirely on the top of stove, fold together and turn out of the dish, than to try to slip it out.

Miss S. E. Barrett.

BAKED OMELET.

Thicken three cups of milk with one scant tablespoonful of corn starch, one tablespoonful of butter and a teaspoonful of salt. When cool add the whites of four eggs beaten very stiff, separately. Pour into a buttered dish, and bake twenty minutes.

G.

☞ *Use SMITH'S COMMON SENSE Baking Powder and True-Fruit Flavoring Extracts. They are the best. See page 5.*

CREAMED EGGS.

Boil six eggs for half an hour; remove the yolks and cut the whites into slices. Heat three cupfuls of milk, and thicken with two heaping tablespoonfuls of flour and one of butter. Rub the yolks to a smooth paste, and mix them with the white sauce gradually. When the yolks are smoothly mixed with the sauce, add the whites, salt and pepper to taste, and pour over slices of buttered toast. M.

BREAKFAST DISH.

Put one-half cup of bread crumbs in a spider with one-half cup of milk, one tablespoonful of butter, some pepper and salt. When the crumbs have absorbed the milk, break in two eggs and stir slightly with the mixture, and then cook like an omelet.

Mrs. W. S. KACHLER.

MEATS.

For roast meats the oven should be very hot the first ten minutes, and more moderate during the rest of the time.

In broiling steak or chops, if the dripping causes the fire to blaze, a clear bed of coals may be obtained by throwing on a little salt.

In boiling, fresh meat should be boiled rapidly the first fifteen minutes, to harden the albumen on the surface and preserve the juices; after that the kettle should be set where it will just simmer.

Boiled mutton will be more juicy if wrapped tightly in a thickly floured piece of coarse cotton.

Every scrap of meat left from roasts and steaks can be used in made dishes, and should never be thrown away.

The tough ends of sirloin and porterhouse steaks should be cut off before broiling and utilized in Hamburg steaks for breakfast the next morning.

Use SMITH'S COMMON SENSE Baking Powder and True-Fruit Flavoring Extracts. They are the best. See page 5.

Some of the most appetizing and nutritious dishes are made with the despised cheap cuts of meat.

The flavor of roast meat is very much improved by using a meat rack in the bottom of the dripping pan, thus preventing the meat from becoming water soaked. The rack may be procured at any hardware store.

RIB ROAST WITH YORKSHIRE PUDDING.

Buy a rib roast and have the butcher remove the bones and roll the meat. Roast fifteen minutes for every pound. Three-quarters of an hour before the meat is done, remove from pan and pour out nearly all the drippings (reserving them for gravy). Turn in the pudding, replace the roast upon the rack, *across*, not in the pan, and complete the roasting. For the pudding, beat three eggs light, add one pint of milk and a pinch of salt. Pour half this mixture on six large tablespoonfuls of flour and beat until smooth, then add the remainder of the mixture, and pour all into the dripping pan. Cut in squares when done and serve as a garnish with the roast. This will serve six.

MRS. W. A. MONTGOMERY.

TO COOK ROUND STEAK.

Cut one slice of round steak into pieces, place in porcelain kettle with one cupful of barley, salt, pepper, and water enough to cover. Bake in the kettle closely covered three or four hours in slow oven.

MRS. A. ELWOOD.

TOAD IN THE HOLE.

One pound round steak, one pint of milk, one cupful of flour, one egg, salt and pepper; cut the steak into dice, beat the egg very light, add milk to it and half a teaspoon of salt. Pour upon the flour gradually, beating very light and smooth. Butter a two-quart dish and put the meat in it, season well and pour the batter over it. Bake an hour in a moderate oven. Serve hot. (Can use mutton or lamb instead of steak.)

MRS. C. CROUCH.

☞ *Use SMITH'S COMMON SENSE Baking Powder and True-Fruit Flavoring Extracts. They are the best. See page 5.*

VEAL LOAF.

One pound raw veal, piece of butter size of egg, three slices of bread, two eggs, one teaspoonful mustard, salt and pepper. Chop meat and bread fine, add eggs beaten, butter, pepper, salt and mustard. Bake two hours.

Mrs. C. E. Crouch.

HAMBURG STEAKS.

Have the butcher mince, very fine, round steak or the tougher portion of the sirloin. To one pound of this minced meat add one tablespoonful of onion juice, half a teaspoonful of salt and a dash of pepper. Mix and form with the hands into round, flat cakes. Heat two tablespoonfuls of butter in a frying pan, put in the steaks and cook rapidly until brown on both sides. Place the steaks on hot platter, add a tablespoonful of flour to the butter in the pan, mix thoroughly, add a cup of boiling water, stir until smooth, add salt and pepper and, if desired, a spoonful of mushroom catsup or Worcestershire sauce, pour over the steaks and serve. One pound will make eight Hamburgs. They may be broiled if preferred.

M.

BEEF STEW WITH DUMPLINGS.

One pound of lean meat from the shoulder, cut into small bits, dredge with flour, brown in frying pan in drippings or butter. Skim out the meat when browned over, add one pint of water and one tablespoonful of flour to the butter or drippings remaining in the frying pan. Put back the meat with a slice of onion and sprig of parsley, cover the frying pan and *simmer* for two hours.

To make the dumplings, take one cupful of flour, one large teaspoonful of baking powder, and enough milk to make a soft dough. If necessary, add a little water to the stew to make a good gravy; season, dip up the dumplings by spoonfuls and place on top the stew; cover, simmer for ten minutes and serve immediately. Do not uncover until the dumplings are done or they will be heavy.

H. B. M.

☞ *Use SMITH'S COMMON SENSE Baking Powder and True-Fruit Flavoring Extracts. They are the best. See page 5.*

BOSTON HASH.

Place in a baking dish a layer of cold mashed potatoes, then one of finely-chopped meat ; have the last layer potato ; pour over one cupful of milk (scant), dot with butter, salt and pepper; bake in quick oven until brown.

MRS. ALVARADO STEVENS.

RISSOLES.

To two cupfuls of finely chopped cold meat, add two table-spoonfuls of water, one of butter, a dash of salt and pepper ; when boiling, stir in one well-beaten egg, and remove from the fire. Roll out pieces of tender pie crust, until about five inches in diameter ; place a spoonful of the mixture on the crust at one side of the center, fold over like a turnover, pinch the edges together ; bake in a quick oven twenty minutes.

W. A. M.

CROQUETTES.

Croquettes may be made of *any kind* of cold meat chopped *very, very* fine.

Any quantity of meat may be used, by remembering the general rule, to use just half as much milk or cream as you have meat, and to make the mixture as soft as it can be handled.

In measuring the quantity of meat, always press solidly into the cup.

To shape croquettes, place the hot mixture by spoonfuls on some shallow dish or platter, using a large cooking spoon and giving each spoonful as nearly cylindrical shape as possible. Do not be troubled if the mixture spreads ; it will be stiff enough when cold. When perfectly cold, take these spoonfuls from the platter with a pancake turner, and shape with the hands lightly ; dip the croquette into beaten egg, remove on the pancake turner, roll in very fine bread crumbs until a perfect cylinder, and lay at one side of your board. In frying, place several in a wire frying basket, and brown in boiling fat; drain on brown paper.

After making a few times, croquettes are very quickly and easily shaped ; they may be set away for a day before frying

---

☞ *Use SMITH'S COMMON SENSE Baking Powder and True-Fruit Flavoring Extracts. They are the best. See page 5.*

if desired. If properly made they should be creamy within and not at all greasy.

If one has no frying basket croquettes may be slipped from the pancake turner into the boiling fat, and taken out on the same useful little article.

CHICKEN CROQUETTES.

Boil one cupful of cream or milk, add one heaping tablespoonful of butter, two cupfuls of finely chopped chicken, two tablespoonfuls of flour, salt, pepper, and, if desired, a teaspoonful each of onion and lemon juice, and a finely minced sprig of parsley. Let the mixture boil two minutes, add two beaten eggs and remove from the fire. Many use half sweetbread and half chicken in making chicken croquettes. To obtain onion juice, grate on a coarse grater.

MRS. W. A. MONTGOMERY.

SWEETBREADS.

In buying sweetbreads, be sure to get veal sweetbread, as that from beef is tough. After removing the fibrous skin, parboil in granite or porcelain kettle fifteen minutes in water that just simmers, and then throw them into cold water. They should be parboiled as soon as received, as they spoil quickly. Sweetbreads, at most seasons of the year, are an economical as well as delicious article of diet.

BROILED SWEETBREADS.

Parboil, split, butter thickly, and broil over clear fire until a delicate brown. Serve on hot platter with border of fried apples, or fry in hot saucepan with butter.

SWEETBREAD PATTIES.

Parboil one pair of sweetbreads thoroughly; chop fine with a silver knife. Make a cream sauce with one coffee cup of cream, one tablespoonful of butter and one tablespoonful of flour. Into this stir the sweetbreads, the white of one hard-boiled egg chopped fine, and the yolks of two creamed, gradually into the sauce. Care must be taken to boil the eggs until the yolks are

---

☞ *Use SMITH'S COMMON SENSE Baking Powder and True-Fruit Flavoring Extracts. They are the best. See page 5.*

perfectly dry and creamy or they will not blend with the sauce. Add salt and a dash of white pepper. Let all cook gently five minutes, then place a spoonful of the mixture into little shells of puff pastry, and serve at once. These are very nice for luncheon served with French pease.

MRS. W. A. MONTGOMERY.

BAKED SWEETBREADS.

Parboil, dredge with flour, salt and pepper, lay on a meat rack in a baking pan, cover the bottom with water, and bake in a moderate oven forty minutes. Make a sauce with one cupful of milk or cream ; into it pour one cupful of French pease, drained of their liquor, heat, serve the sweetbread on a hot platter and pour over it the dressing. W. A. M.

BRAISING.

Braising is a combination of roasting and boiling, in which meat is partially covered with boiling water, and then roasted in a tightly-covered pan. This method possesses many advantages, for pieces of meat otherwise tough and tasteless, when braised are appetizing and nutritious. The essentials in braising are to have the pan tightly covered, the pores of the meat closed by browning in hot drippings before putting in the water, and enough vegetables used to impart flavor and prevent dryness. Pieces from the shoulder, flank and rump of beef, mutton or veal, also tongue and calves liver, are especially good braised.

BRAISED LAMB.

In the bottom of the braising pan, heat a little fat or drippings ; in this fry one small onion ; put in the piece of lamb to be braised, and brown on all sides. Remove the lamb, and slice into the pan one raw potato, one stalk of celery, and one small carrot ; add a spoonful of mushroom catsup or Worcestershire sauce, if desired, with salt and pepper. Replace the lamb on a meat rack, half cover with boiling water, cover tightly, and roast in moderate oven until very tender. Let the liquid cook down, and pour over the lamb before serving.

☞ *Use SMITH'S COMMON SENSE Baking Powder and True-Fruit Flavoring Extracts. They are the best. See page 5.*

BRAISED TONGUE.

Put one fresh beef's tongue in kettle, cover with boiling water, simmer for two hours. After skinning the tongue, roll it and tie, place it on a meat rack in a deep baking pan, and pour around it a sauce made as follows: Put two tablespoonfuls of butter in a frying pan, let it brown, stir into it two tablespoonfuls of flour, mix, add one quart of water in which the tongue was boiled, one raw potato sliced, one onion, one stalk of celery, one carrot, and, if desired, a tablespoonful of mushroom catsup, and a sprig of parsley. When the sauce boils, pour into the baking pan, cover tightly, and bake two hours, basting every half hour. Dish the tongue on a platter, and pour around it the sauce. MRS. STEVENS.

MOCK DUCK OR BRAISED BEEF.

Cover one thick slice of round steak evenly with a bread crumb dressing, roll tightly and tie. Brown the entire surface of the roll in a hot frying pan in a little butter or drippings; then place the roll in the baking pan with enough *boiling* water to nearly cover it; bake slowly until the liquor is cooked down to a thick gravy. Pour over the roll, and serve either hot or cold.
MRS. SERVOSS.

PRESSED CHICKEN.

Cook a chicken until the meat drops from the bones. Cut the meat into small pieces, return the skin and bones to the kettle, and boil until the liquor is reduced to about a pint; strain, season to taste, adding chopped mushrooms, if desired; mix with the chicken and put all in a mould. Place a flat cover on it and press with a light weight over night. Turn out from the mould, garnish with lemon and parsley, and serve.

CHICKEN IN JELLY.

Prepare two chickens as for fricassee; skim thoroughly just before they boil; when tender remove the white meat from the bones. Make a jelly of one-third box of gelatine soaked in one cupful of water one hour, one pint of chicken broth free from grease and sediment, juice of two lemons and grated rind of one,

---

☞ *Use SMITH'S COMMON SENSE Baking Powder and True-Fruit Flavoring Extracts. They are the best. See page 5.*

one-fourth cupful of white sugar. Boil five minutes before adding the lemon, strain, and when cold, but not set, arrange in it the chicken cut in various shaped pieces. When hardened, remove from mould, garnish with nasturtium blossoms.

Mrs. Desmond.

FILLET OF VEAL WITH FORCE MEAT.

Remove the bone from a fillet of veal, and stuff with the following force meat: One bowlful of grated bread crumbs, a little sweet marjoram, lemon peel, thyme and parsley, one-half cupful of scraped bacon, or the same quantity of butter. Chop and mix with one raw egg and one cupful of sweet cream. Season to taste with salt and cayenne. Make another force meat of one quart of oysters, one pint of rolled cracker, one-half cupful of butter and one cupful of chopped celery; salt, add cayenne to taste. Make cuts in the outside of the fillet, and stuff each cut with this force meat. Tie the fillet and cover with a thin paste that can be removed, and bake.

Mrs. Desmond.

MUTTON À LA VENISON.

Tak a leg of mutton and lard it well with strips of salt pork inserted in deep slits in the meat, which has been previously rolled in pepper and cloves; bake two hours, or according to the size of the roast, basting frequently while in the oven. About an hour before serving, spread over it currant jelly, return to the oven and let it brown.

Mrs. Sinclair.

BOILED HAM.

Put the ham into a kettle nearly full of cold water, and let it come to a boil on the back of the stove ; this should take two hours. Skim, and let it stand where it will *simmer* gently fifteen minutes to every pound. Let it cool in the water in which it boiled. In boiling a half ham, plaster the side from which slices have been cut thickly with moistened corn meal, sew in a cloth and boil. This will prevent the meat from drying.

Mrs. A. S. Montgomery.

☞ *Use SMITH'S COMMON SENSE Baking Powder and True-Fruit Flavoring Extracts. They are the best. See page 5.*

MADE DISH WITH HAM.

Spread bread dice with butter, then lightly with made mustard, cover with a deep layer of cheese and ham. Fry in butter, without turning, lift out and set in a hot oven for four minutes.

MRS. DESMOND.

TO COOK VERY SALT HAM.

Soak sliced ham that is too salt, in sweet milk over night. Fry the ham and remove from the spider, turn off most of the drippings, stir into the remainder one tablespoonful of flour, and add the milk in which the ham was soaked. Thicken, pour around the ham, after placing scrambled eggs on each slice.

MRS. DESMOND.

TONGUE IN JELLY.

Boil and skin a tongue. Cover the bottom of a two quart mould with a jelly made as follows: One quart of beef stock, half a box of gelatine dissolved in a cup of cold water, a tablespoonful of onion juice, a stick of celery chopped fine, salt, a dash of red pepper. Boil the stock, onion and celery for ten minutes, add the gelatine, and as soon as dissolved take from the fire. Strain and pour enough into a mould to cover the bottom. When this has hardened, place the tongue and half a cupful of jelly that has cooled but not thickened ; when hard add the rest of the jelly and set away to harden. When ready to serve, dip the mould in warm water and then turn on a platter. Garnish and serve.

FRIED PORK.

Cut side pork into slices one-eight of an inch thick ; soak in thick sour milk over night. Wash and dry, dust and fry brown. Beat two eggs very light, stir in two tablespoonfuls of flour ; dip the slices of pork in this batter, return immediately to the hot drippings and fry light brown. Serve at once garnished with mashed-potato cones.

MRS. DESMOND.

BROILED KIDNEYS.

Take mutton or veal kidneys and split them in half. Carefully trim all skin and fat from the inside. Season, dip in melted butter and flour, and broil over a clear fire.

☞ *Use SMITH'S COMMON SENSE Baking Powder and True-Fruit Flavoring Extracts. They are the best. See page 5.*

BEEF À LA MODE.

Mix three pounds of finely chopped round steak, raw, with one egg, one slice of bread, one cup sweet milk, one tablespoonful salt, one teaspoonful pepper. Form into a loaf and bake one hour in a slow oven.

Mrs. A. J. Barrett.

TONGUE ON TOAST.

Chop cold boiled tongue very fine, add to one cupful of tongue two eggs beaten, salt, pepper, two tablespoonfuls of boiling water, bring all to a boil, and serve immediately on squares of buttered toast.

ESCALOPED MUTTON.

Put a layer of finely chopped cold mutton in the bottom of a baking dish, then a layer of bread crumbs, then one of stewed tomatoes, bits of butter, salt, pepper; repeat until dish is full, covering the top with crumbs. Bake one hour.   M.

MINT SAUCE.

Chop one bunch of fresh mint very fine and mix with it a teaspoonful of sugar and a pinch of salt. Add one-fourth cup of vinegar, and serve with roast lamb or mutton.

BREAD SAUCE.

Put one pint of milk and one-half pint of bread crumbs into a double kettle, add a tablespoonful of onion juice (extracted by rubbing the onion on a grater), a blade of mace and a bay leaf; boil five minutes, press through a sieve and return to the kettle, add two tablespoonfuls of butter, with salt and pepper to taste, heat thoroughly, and serve with fish or poultry.

Mrs. Makeham.

CELERY SAUCE.

Clean and stew slowly in a pint of water five roots of celery until very tender, then press through a colander and stir it into one pint of milk thickened with one even tablespoonful of flour. Add salt, butter and pepper and serve with boiled fowl.

Mrs. Makeham.

☞ Use *SMITH'S COMMON SENSE* Baking Powder and True-Fruit Flavoring Extracts. They are the best. See page 5.

CREAM SAUCE WITH MUSHROOMS.

Stir together until smooth one tablespoonful each of butter and flour in a hot saucepan, add very carefully and gradually, stirring all the time, a cupful of sweet cream, with salt and pepper to taste. When thickened, add a cupful of either fresh or canned mushrooms chopped fine. If canned, simply heat through, as boiling makes them tough; if fresh, boil ten minutes. Good with sweet breads or fried chicken.

MRS. MAKEHAM.

VEGETABLES.

To render old potatoes mealy, let them lie in cold water an hour or two before cooking.

A scant teaspoonful of soda added to the water in which string beans are to be cooked, will make them tender, and shorten the time of cooking.

Onions will be firmer and of better flavor, if cooked in hard water.

Soft water may be hardened by adding a teaspoonful of salt.

Water should always be boiling before vegetables are placed in it, and should continue to boil until they are done.

Young green vegetables should be cooked in boiling *hard* water to retain their color and flavor.

FRENCH FRIED POTATOES.

Pare raw potatoes and cut them in thick slices; if old or wilted, let them lie in cold water for an hour. Wipe them dry, and fry in a deep kettle of boiling fat for about ten minutes. Drain, salt, and serve. If properly fried, they will be dry and mealy like a baked potato.

MRS. BARRETT.

☞ *Use SMITH'S COMMON SENSE Baking Powder and True-Fruit Flavoring Extracts. They are the best. See page 5.*

POTATO CROQUETTS.

Mix one quart mashed potatoes, one cupful of cream, two eggs, one tablespoonful of butter, and four slices of stale bread; thoroughly season, and make into small rolls. Dip them in cream, and then in flour and corn-meal equal parts. Fry in hot lard.

Mrs. A. Elwood.

FRENCH BAKED POTATOES.

Pare the potatoes and split lengthwise. Spread each piece on the flat side thickly with butter, add a dash of pepper and salt, place the potatoes in a baking pan with boiling water to cover the bottom, and bake in a good oven until golden brown.

Miss. Vic. Crowther.

DELICIOUS SWEET POTATOES.

Pare the potatoes and divide if very large; place in granite or porcelain kettle with just enough boiling water to cover; add one tablespoonful of sugar, and two of butter for each half dozen large potatoes. Boil for half an hour, remove the potatoes and lay in a baking dish. Pour the liquor remaining over them, and bake to a rich brown, basting occasionally.

Miss Crowther.

ESCALOPED POTATOES.

Boil twelve good sized potatoes, cut into dice. Put into a deep dish a layer of potatoes, sprinkle liberally with butter, salt and pepper, then another layer of potatoes, until the dish is nearly full. Cover the top with rolled cracker and bits of butter, fill the dish with milk and cream, and bake two hours slowly while covered, then remove cover, and brown.

Mrs. H. C. Williams.

ESCALOPED POTATOES.

Make a sauce with one pint milk, two tablespoonfuls of flour and two of butter, mix smoothly, salt and pepper to taste. Put a layer of this into the bottom of a baking dish, then a layer of boiled potatoes sliced thin, and so on, having the last layer sauce. Sprinkle with fine bread crumbs, and brown in a hot oven. This quantity of sauce is enough for four large potatoes.

☞ Use *SMITH'S COMMON SENSE Baking Powder and True-Fruit Flavoring Extracts. They are the best. See page* 5.

STUFFED POTATOES.

Cut the tops off from six large baked potatoes as soon as they are done. Take out the inside carefully, so as not to break the skin, into a hot basin. Mash until light with cream, butter and salt, beating them until snow white; add the stiffly beaten white of an egg, return the mixture to the skins, heaping it on top. Brush over with the yolk of an egg and brown in a hot oven. This is an excellent way to save baked potatoes from becoming watery, if for any reason dinner is delayed.

Dr. Sherman.

POTATO PUFFS.

Stir into two cupfuls of mashed potatoes, two tablespoonfuls of butter, beating to a white cream. Add two beaten eggs, a teacup of cream or milk, and salt to taste. Bake until golden brown.

Mrs. Servoss.

CREAMED POTATOES.

Thicken milk, and season as for milk toast. Slice cold boiled potatoes, heat them thoroughly in the milk and serve.

Mrs. W. S. Kachler.

TO COOK CELERY.

Cut up the outer stalks of celery into small pieces, boil in granite kettle one hour, drain, season with salt, pepper and butter, add one cup of milk and thicken slightly with flour.

Mrs. A. Elwood.

FRENCH BAKED APPLE.

Pare, quarter and core large fine apples. On each quarter lay a piece of butter and a teaspoonful of sugar. Place in a baking dish with a very little water; bake until transparent and delicately browned. Serve as a garnish with meats.

Miss Victoria Crowther.

BAKED PEARS.

Take a small stone jar, such as is used for baking beans, fill it with alternate layers of pears, halved but not pared, and sugar. Fill the jar with water, cover, and bake three hours in a moderate oven.

☞ *Use SMITH'S COMMON SENSE Baking Powder and True-Fruit Flavoring Extracts. They are the best. See page 5.*

BOSTON BAKED BEANS.

Pick and wash one quart of beans, put in cold water and cook until the skin cracks open when you blow on them. Drain out of this water into a deep earthen jar or crock, with half a pound of salt pork scored across the top. Bake slowly eight hours, keeping covered with boiling water until nearly done, when the water should be allowed to cook down. Many add a tablespoonful of molasses.

Miss S. R. TAYLOR.

CORN OYSTERS.

Chop enough uncooked green corn fine to make two cupfuls; add two beaten eggs and one teaspoonful of baking powder, one cupful of milk, and flour enough to make a good batter. Fry in a well greased hot spider in spoonfuls to make about the size of a fried oyster.

Miss NELLIE KISHLAR.

CORN PIE.

Cut from the cob four ears of cold boiled corn, add to it two-thirds cupful of milk, a small piece of butter, salt, pepper, and two eggs beaten separately, and a teaspoonful of corn starch. Bake in two pie tins in a quick oven.

BAKED OR STUFFED ONIONS.

For this use the Spanish or some large onion. Boil for one hour or longer, if very large, then set in baking pan with a little water, put a piece of butter on each one, and sprinkle with crumbs, bake until tender, at least one hour. Serve with a cream sauce. If the onions are to be stuffed, remove the heart after boiling, and fill the center with minced meat, highly seasoned, then bake as above.

Mrs. M.

WINTER SQUASH.

Cut in three inch squares, scrape off the soft part, place the squares in a baking dish, put a small piece of butter on each, salt and pepper, bake until tender. Serve it on the shell, a square to each person. The squash may be cut in half, and a spoonful helped to each person.

☞ Use *SMITH'S COMMON SENSE Baking Powder and True-Fruit Flavoring Extracts. They are the best. See page 5.*

BAKED TOMATOES.

Cut a slice from the stem end of large, firm tomatoes; with the fingers carefully remove the center of the tomato. Make a force meat of finely minced ham or veal, bread crumbs, salt, pepper, butter, and fill the tomato, rounding the top and sprinkling with bread crumbs. Put the tomatoes in a granite baking pan in which is a very little water, bake forty minutes in hot oven, take up carefully on a cake turner, and serve.

M.

FRIED TOMATOES.

Cut in thick slices without peeling, dip the slices either in batter or egg and bread crumbs, and fry until brown in buttered sauce-pan.

TOMATOES AND MACARONI.

Break six sticks of macaroni into short lengths, boil until tender in salted water, drain, and pour over it one quart of canned tomatoes, season, let come to a boil and serve. This is very good escaloped, using one layer of macaroni to one of stewed tomato, covering with bread crumbs and browning in a hot oven.

MRS. A. S. MONTGOMERY.

FRIED PARSNIPS.

Boil the parsnips until tender and mash, adding to a pint of mashed parsnip, a large tablespoonful of butter, two tablespoonfuls of milk or cream, pepper, salt. When the mixture is very hot, add a well beaten egg, and remove from the fire. When cool, make into small balls, dip in egg, and then in bread crumbs, fry in kettle of hot lard.

COLD SLAW.

One quart of cut cabbage, two eggs, one-half cup of cream; (sour is best), one teaspoonful of salt, two tablespoonfuls of vinegar, a little pepper, butter the size of a walnut. Cut the cabbage very fine, and put in bowl. Put the vinegar on to boil. Beat the eggs until light, add to them the cream and butter. Now add to these the boiling vinegar, stir over the fire until boiling hot, add the salt and pepper, and pour over the cabbage and it is ready to serve when cold.

MRS. MAKEHAM.

Use SMITH'S COMMON SENSE Baking Powder and True-Fruit Flavoring Extracts. They are the best. See page 5.

SALADS.

Use silver or wooden spoon in preparing salad dressing.
Have all the ingredients very cold.
Never mix any salad with its dressing until just ready to serve.
With a little ingenuity many salads not in the books, but yet wholesome and delicious, may be concocted from the bits left over.

FRENCH DRESSING.

Place one-half teaspoonful of salt, and one-fourth teaspoonful of black pepper in a bowl, and then stir in gradually three tablespoonfuls of pure olive oil, and little by little one tablespoonful of strong vinegar; mix thoroughly. This is used with a plain lettuce salad, with water-cress, endive or nasturtium blossoms; sprinkled over the salad just before serving.

W. A. M.

MAYONNAISE DRESSING.

One tablespoonful of mustard, one tablespoonful of sugar, one dash of cayenne, one teaspoonful of salt, yolks of two uncooked eggs, juice of one-half lemon, one-fourth cupful of vinegar, three-fourth pint of salad oil. Beat the yolks and dry ingredients until thick, add the oil slowly until very thick, then the vinegar and oil alternately, and last the lemon juice. A cupful of whipped cream is an improvement, but the beaten whites of the eggs may be used instead; add the cream or whites beaten just before using. This will keep in a cool place several weeks. Everything used in making this dressing must be ice cold. If the oil and eggs should curdle, begin with more fresh yolks in another dish as directed, and add the curdled dressing gradually.

Mrs. W. A. Montgomery.

SALAD DRESSING WITHOUT OIL.

Four eggs, one tablespoonful of salt, one cup of butter, one cup of mustard, one-half cup of sugar, one cup of cream, a

---

☞ *Use SMITH'S COMMON SENSE Baking Powder and True-Fruit Flavoring Extracts. They are the best. See page 5.*

little cayenne pepper. Cook over boiling water. Remove from the fire and stir in one pint of vinegar.

MRS. FRANK UPTON.

SALAD DRESSING WITH OIL.

Six eggs, two teaspoonfuls of sugar, four and one-half teaspoonfuls of salt, four and one-half teaspoonfuls of mustard, three tablespoonfuls of cream, one teacupful of vinegar. Cook over boiling water until thick. When cold add a drop at a time —six tablespoonfuls of olive oil.

MRS. FRANK UPTON.

SALAD DRESSING.

One tablespoonful each of mustard, sugar, salt, butter, one and one-half tablespoonfuls of flour. Beat all together; add three well-beaten eggs, one-half cup of vinegar, one-half cup of water, and last, one cup of cream or milk. Cook fifteen minutes; stirring constantly.

MRS. GEO. W. HERR.

SALAD DRESSING, TO KEEP.

Two boiled potatoes, put through a sieve, one teaspoonful of mustard flour, two of salt, a dash of cayenne, one raw egg; mix, then add yolks of three hard-boiled eggs, six tablespoonfuls of olive oil or melted butter, eight of vinegar, three of white sugar, four of sweet cream, and the white of an egg beaten stiff. Bottle and set in a cool place, and it will keep for months. For meat salad, to one cupful of this dressing, add the beaten whites of two eggs, and one cupful of whipped cream.

MRS. DESMOND.

SALAD DRESSING, FOR IMMEDIATE USE.

Place a deep dish in snow or cracked ice, break into it one egg and the whites of two, beat with an egg beater until they begin to rope, then add gradually one pint of olive oil. Beat to a paste the hard-boiled yolks of four eggs; mix with them one tablespoonful of mustard which has been cooked one-half hour in five tablespoonfuls of water, four tablespoonfuls of vinegar, one-half tablespoonful of salt and a dash of cayenne. Have

---

☞ *Use SMITH'S COMMON SENSE Baking Powder and True-Fruit Flavoring Extracts. They are the best. See page 5.*

ready this last mixture before beginning, and add it gradually to to the contents of the bowl. Last add one-half cup of sweet cream and the beaten whites of two eggs.

Mrs. Desmond.

DRESSING FOR CHICKEN SALAD.

Mix together two tablespoonfuls of flour, one of butter and one cupful of moderately strong vinegar; place in bowl and set in boiling water. Then add one well beaten egg, one teaspoonful of mustard, a little salt; boil until smooth and thin with cream when cold.

Miss Hattie Skinner.

SOUR CREAM SALAD DRESSING.

Mix thoroughly one cupful of rich, sour cream with one teaspoonful each of salt and sugar, a dash cayenne, three tablespoonfuls of vinegar. Good with cabbage and cauliflower.

M.

CAULIFLOWER SALAD.

Boil one small cauliflower until tender, lay in cold water until wanted. Pick it apart into small pieces, dry carefully on a towel, put in a salad dish and pour on it one cupful of mayonnaise dressing. Let it stand about a quarter of an hour and serve.

Mrs. Makeham.

CABBAGE SALAD.

Two teaspoonfuls of salt, two and one-half of mustard, one of flour, one-half cup of sugar, one egg, butter the size of a walnut. Mix together and add three tablespoonfuls of milk and one-half cup of vinegar. Cook well, stirring all the time; when cool pour over finely chopped cabbage.

Mrs. W. S. Kachler.

CHICKEN SALAD.

Cut cold roast or boiled chicken into dice, and if a very elegant salad is desired, use only the white meat. Season with salt and pepper and set away in a cold place until needed. Cut into pieces half an inch thick, tender, white celery, two-thirds the

---

☞ *Use SMITH'S COMMON SENSE Baking Powder and True-Fruit Flavoring Extracts. They are the best. See page 5.*

quantity of the chicken, put in a bowl, cover with towel wet in ice water, and set in the refrigerator. When ready to serve, mix the chicken and celery, being sure that the celery is carefully dried if it has been put in water at all. Pour over the mayonnaise dressing, allowing one cup and a-half to each pint of chicken. Garnish with celery tips, and serve immediately.

MRS. BIGELOW.

LOBSTER SALAD.

Mince the lobster as directed for chicken salad. Arrange two or three crisp white lettuce leaves together shell shape, and place these shells on a platter. Mix the lobster with mayonnaise, place a spoonful in each shell, and add a teaspoonful of dressing over all. If in season, a nasturtium blossom laid in each shell makes a pretty garnish.

MRS. W. A. MONTGOMERY.

FISH SALAD.

Salmon, or any cold boiled fish, may be used as salad, arranged with lettuce as directed for lobster salad. Plainer dressing may be used.

M.

SWEETBREAD SALAD.

Prepare as directed for lobster salad. Delicious.

CELERY SALAD.

Cut tender white celery into half-inch pieces, and to every pint allow a half of mayonnaise or other dressing. Serve immediately after mixing with Bismark or Newport wafers.

H. B.

EGG SALAD.

On a crisp leaf of lettuce, slice one-half a hard boiled egg. Cover with a spoonful of mayonnaise, and serve with cheese straws or toasted crackers.

W. A. M.

POTATO SALAD.

Chop five cold-boiled potatoes with one small onion and a little parsley until very fine; salt to taste. Mash the yolks of two hard-boiled eggs perfectly smooth, and add one teaspoonful

---

☞ *Use SMITH'S COMMON SENSE Baking Powder and True-Fruit Flavoring Extracts. They are the best. See page 5.*

of dry mustard, a dash of cayenne pepper, two tablespoonfuls of salad oil and five of vinegar ; mix thoroughly. Pour over the potatoes an hour before using, garnish with the whites of egg and parsley.

Mrs. W. A. Morrison.

Potato salad may also be made with any of the salad dressings given.

TOMATO SALAD.

Peel small and perfectly smooth tomatoes, slicing them nearly through, but letting them retain their shape. Place on ice. When ready to serve, place each tomato in a shell of lettuce leaves and pour over it a large spoonful of mayonnaise dressing.

M.

BREAD, BREAKFAST CAKES, ETC.

HOP YEAST.

Two even teacupfuls of sifted flour, two medium sized potatoes, boiled and mashed through a colander, one heaping teaspoonful each of sugar and salt; put all into a crock. Boil one teacupful of hops in three pints of water, for twenty minutes, strain while still boiling into the contents of the crock, and mix until smooth. When cool, add one cake of yeast, let it rise and stir it down. Cover and put in a cool place. It will keep several weeks. One cupful should be saved each time to make new yeast with.

Mrs. J. Handy.

SALT RISING BREAD.

Pour a pint of boiling water in a two-quart pail or pitcher, on a half tablespoonful of salt; when the finger can be held in it, add flour enough to make a thick batter, and beat vigorously until full of air bubbles. Cover, stand in a pan of warm water,

---

☞ *Use SMITH'S COMMON SENSE Baking Powder and True-Fruit Flavoring Extracts. They are the best. See page 5.*

and keep in a warm place over night. In the morning this sponge should be very light, and of a peculiar odor. Mix this salt rising with a stiff batter made of one pint of scalded milk, and enough flour so that it will just drop from a spoon. Beat until smooth, cover, and set in a pan of warm water until light; add flour to make a dough, mould thoroughly, make into loaves, and when very light, bake.

Mrs. A. S. Montgomery.

ENGLISH BISCUITS.

One and a half pints of flour, one coffeecupful corn starch, three tablespoonfuls sugar, large pinch salt, two teaspoonfuls baking powder, three tablespoonfuls lard, one egg, one-half pint milk, one-half cup currants, one tablespoonful coriander seed (if desired). Sift together flour, corn starch, sugar, salt, and powder, rub in the lard (cold); add eggs beaten, milk, currants well washed, picked and dried, and coriander seeds. Mix into smooth dough, soft enough to handle. Flour the board, roll out the dough one-fourth inch thick, and cut with a large round cutter; lay them on greased baking tin, and bake in rather hot oven twenty minutes. Rub over with little butter on clean piece of linen, when taken from oven.

Miss M. Pearce.

RAISED BISCUITS OR ROLLS.

One pint sweet milk scalding hot, one-fourth teacup of sugar, one-half teacup of butter, one small teaspoonful of salt. Put these into the milk while hot; *when cool*, stir in the white of one egg, well beaten, and one compressed yeast cake dissolved in a little water. Then add enough sifted flour to make a stiff batter, and let rise till very light ; work in flour to make soft dough, and let rise again. When very light, form into small rolls or buscuits, let rise very light, and rub over the tops with a little warm milk and butter, and bake in a quick oven. This receipt makes about thirty medium sized buscuits.

Mrs. Miller.

RAISED BISCUITS OR ROLLS.

Boil two good sized potatoes, scald two tablespoonfuls each of flour and sugar with the water in which the potatoes

---

☞ *Use SMITH'S COMMON SENSE Baking Powder and True-Fruit Flavoring Extracts. They are the best. See page 5.*

were boiled. Add to this the mashed potatoes and enough water to make with that used in scalding the flour, two cupfuls. When this mixture is cool, add one-third of a yeast cake dissolved in a little water. Stand this sponge in a moderately warm place over night. In the morning add one cup of warm water, a little salt, and flour to make a thick sponge. Let this rise, add flour to make a soft dough, knead fifteen minutes. Let rise again, then add one-third cupful of mixed butter and lard, mix thoroughly, let rise until very light; mould into biscuits, and when very light, bake in a moderate oven.

Mrs. S. A. Ellis.

BROWN BREAD

Mix together two cupfuls of corn meal, one of flour, two of sour milk, one-half cupful of molasses, two even spoonfuls of soda, and one of salt. Pour into a thoroughly greased two-quart basin and steam three hours.

Miss Taylor.

BOSTON BROWN BREAD.

Make a batter of three teacupfuls of corn meal, two of graham flour, one of molasses, and three and one-half of warm water, with one full teaspoonful of soda. Steam for three hours.

Mrs. A. S. Montgomery.

PARKER HOUSE ROLLS.

Scald one pint of milk, add three teaspoonfuls of sugar, one of salt, one half teacupful of lard or butter. When slightly cool, add a compressed yeast cake and flour to make a stiff sponge, and when light, mix as for bread. Let it rise again until very light, then mould until free from air bubbles, roll until two-thirds of an inch thick, cut out with tin cutter, brush with melted butter and fold. When very light, bake in quick oven. Where compressed yeast is used, these may be set in the morning to be ready for tea, or with slower yeast may be set the night before. In hot weather, one-half a compressed yeast cake is enough.

Mrs. Almstead.

☞ Use *SMITH'S COMMON SENSE Baking Powder and True-Fruit Flavoring Extracts. They are the best. See page 5.*

DELICATE MUFFINS.

One cupful of sweet milk; sift into it two scant cupfuls of flour, mixed with one teaspoonful of salt and three teaspoonfuls of baking powder. Bake in well greased muffin rings in a *hot* oven. If not mixed too stiff, and properly baked, these are exceedingly tender and delicious, and hygienic as well.

Miss S. E. Barrett.

GRAHAM BREAD.

Stir one cupful of graham flour into one pint of boiling water, add one pint of cold water, and enough graham to make a thick batter. Now add two cupfuls of white bread sponge; stand until light; add one cup of molasses, salt, graham to make very stiff batter, pour into pans and let it rise. Bake in slow oven.

RYE BREAD.

One coffeecupful of rye flour, one of wheat, one of corn meal; mix with one and one-half pints of sour milk, two-thirds cupful of molasses, two teaspoonfuls of soda, and two of salt. Steam three hours.

Mrs. Jas. A. Aldridge

STEAMED GRAHAM BREAD.

Mix one and one-half cupfuls each of wheat and graham flour, with two teaspoonfuls of baking powder. Stir into this two cupfuls of sweet milk, and a half cupful of molasses mixed with one-half teaspoonful of soda. Steam three hours, and bake fifteen minutes.

Mrs. Hiram Doty.

MUFFINS.

One quart of flour mixed with two teaspoonfuls of baking powder, one of salt, and one of sugar if desired. Add one pint of milk, and two well beaten eggs. Bake in muffin rings on a griddle or in the oven.

Mrs. Dr. E. S. Jones.

☞ *Use SMITH'S COMMON SENSE Baking Powder and True-Fruit Flavoring Extracts. They are the best. See page 5.*

MUFFINS.

One teacup of milk, one egg, one tablespoon of sugar, one tablespoon of butter, two teaspoons of baking powder, and a little salt. Rub butter and sugar together (as for cake), add the egg, well beaten, mix the baking powder through part of the flour, add the milk, then stir the flour in carefully; make a little stiffer than for cake—about a cup and one-half of flour. Bake in a quick oven in small tins or gem irons.

M. L. JUDSON.

GRAHAM GEMS.

One cupful of sweet milk, one cupful of sifted graham flour, one egg, and one-fourth teaspoonful of salt. Beat very light and bake in gem irons which are hissing hot when the batter is dropped in.

MRS. A. FOULD.

GRAHAM GEMS.

One cupful of graham, one of wheat flour, one teaspoonful of sugar, two-thirds cup of butter, one egg, one even teaspoon of soda, one of salt.

MRS. ALMSTEAD.

BAKED CORN BREAD.

Two cupfuls of corn meal, two cupfuls of flour, one-half cupful each of sugar and butter, three teaspoonfuls of baking powder. Add cold water enough to make a stiff batter, and bake in a very hot oven.

MRS. A. FOULDS.

RAISED DOUGHNUTS.

One and one-half cupfuls of lard, one pint of milk, one pint of water, four eggs, one quart of sugar, one-half teaspoonful of salt, two-thirds cupful of yeast. Melt the lard into the milk, add water, scald; add salt, yeast, one-half of the sugar, and flour to make a stiff batter. Let it stand from noon until bedtime; then add the rest of the sugar, the eggs, and a pinch of soda, and flour enough to make a dough. Mould into a loaf. In the morning roll and cut, let rise on the board. When half risen, turn the cakes over, and when light, fry.

MRS. SERVOSS.

☞ *Use SMITH'S COMMON SENSE Baking Powder and True-Fruit Flavoring Extracts. They are the best. See page 5.*

TEA CAKES OR WIGS.

Two pounds of flour, one-half pound butter well rubbed in, mix with or without one egg. Add four spoonfuls of yeast, a gill of milk—new milk—warm. Let it stand an hour before the fire to rise, after which beat with wooden spoon. Add one-half pound of sugar, a few currants or carraway seeds; with the spoon lift into tins or rings; let stand one-half hour to rise, and bake. Do not kneed with hands as for bread.

MRS. T. H. PATTISON.

POP OVERS.

One teacup of milk, one teacup of sifted flour, one egg, and a little salt. Mix the flour carefully with the milk, add your well beaten egg, and stir thoroughly before dropping into the tins. Have the small tins hot, drop in a small piece of butter, and a tablespoon of the batter. Bake in a moderately quick oven. If too hot, they will not rise nor pop over. They require neither baking powder nor soda.

MRS. LEE JUDSON.

QUICK WAFFLES.

Beat light the yolks of three eggs, add one pint of milk, then three cupfuls of flour, and a pinch of salt; beat until smooth. Add one tablespoon of melted butter, two heaping teapoonfuls of baking powder, and the stiff beaten whites of three eggs. Bake in waffle iron well greased, over clear, hot fire.

MRS. J. W. BROOKS.

SALLY LUM.

Make a batter of one pint of flour, half pint of sweet milk, butter size of an egg, three even teaspoons of sugar, three teaspoons of baking powder, and two eggs. Whip the yolks, add milk, flour, baking powder, sugar, then the butter melted, and last, the whites beaten stiff. Bake twenty minutes in quick oven.

MRS. MILLER.

SPIDER CORN CAKE.

Mix three-fourths cup corn meal, one-fourth cup white flour, one tablespoon of sugar, one-half teaspoon of salt. Beat in one

---

☞ *Use SMITH'S COMMON SENSE Baking Powder and True-Fruit Flavoring Extracts. They are the best. See page 5.*

egg, one-half cup of sour milk, one-fourth cup of sweet milk, one teaspoon of soda. Butter a hot spider, pour in the mixture, then turn over it, but do not stir in, one-fourth cup of sweet milk. Bake in a hot oven.

Mrs. Miller.

FRIED CAKES.

One coffeecupful sour milk, one teacupful of sugar, two eggs, one full teaspoonful of soda, three tablespoonfuls of melted butter, nutmeg, flour to make a soft dough.

Mrs. A. S. Montgomery.

FRIED CAKES.

Beat two eggs light, add one even cupful of sugar, beat until very light; add three even tablespoonfuls of melted lard, beat, add one cupful of sweet milk. Let this stand a few minutes, and stir until the sugar is thoroughly melted before adding the flour, as this prevents the cakes from soaking fat in frying. Sift into this mixture three even teaspoonfuls of baking powder, mixed with enough flour to make a soft dough. Roll out and fry in hot lard.

Mrs. A. J. Barrett.

FRENCH CRULLERS.

Into a cupful of boiling water, put two tablespoonfuls of butter. When it boils, add eight rounded tablespoonfuls of flour, stir over the fire until the dough cleaves from the side of the saucepan. Remove from the fire and beat thoroughly, then stand aside for a half-hour. Add one unbeaten egg, and beat the mixture until smooth; add three other eggs one at a time, beating the whole until very light. Have ready a kettle of clear hot fat, and a plate of pulverized sugar mixed with a little cinnamon. Flour the baking-board and drop on it one tablespoonful of the dough; roll until a quarter of an inch thick, and cut out with a fried cake cutter; lift carefully with a cake turner, slide into the hot fat and brown, drain, and roll in sugar and cinnamon. Troublesome, but delicious.

☞ *Use SMITH'S COMMON SENSE Baking Powder and True-Fruit Flavoring Extracts. They are the best. See page 5.*

RICE PANCAKES.

To one cupful of boiled rice, add one pint of sweet milk, one egg, salt, one tablespoonful of melted butter, two heaping teaspoonfuls of baking powder, mixed with flour enough to make a thin batter.

C. L. M.

CORN MEAL GRIDDLE CAKES.

Make a batter of one pint of buttermilk, one-half cupful of flour, and one of corn meal, one egg, a pinch of salt, and a small teaspoonful of soda dissolved in a little boiling water.

Mrs. A. Elwood.

GRAHAM GRIDDLE CAKES.

Scald one pint of milk, and let it cool, then add two cups of graham flour, one-half cupful of wheat flour, one tablespoonful of compressed yeast dissolved in a little water; beat until smooth. Stand in a warm place over night; in the morning beat two eggs separately, add first the yolks and then the whites. Bake on hot griddle.

M.

BUCKWHEAT CAKES.

Make a smooth thick batter of buckwheat and cold water, add salt and half a compressed yeast cake; stand over night. In the morning thin with milk to required consistency, add one-half teaspoonful of soda in a tablespoonful of boiling water; bake on hot griddle. If water only is used, a tablespoonful of molasses will be required to make the cakes brown evenly.

GRAHAM CRACKERS.

One cupful of milk, and one-half cup of cream, mix with graham to make a soft dough. Knead fifteen minutes, and roll very thin, cut square or round, and bake twenty minutes.

OATMEAL SNAPS.

Mix fine oatmeal with one cupful of sweet cream till stiff; knead slightly, roll *very* thin, cut out, bake until crisp in a slow oven.

☞ *Use SMITH'S COMMON SENSE Baking Powder and True-Fruit Flavoring Extracts. They are the best. See page 5.*

FRUIT CRACKERS.

Make a dough very stiff with one cup of cream and equal parts white and graham flour, with one-half teaspoonful of baking powder sifted in. Roll very thin, cover thickly with dried currants, lay on another sheet of dough, press lightly together, and cut in square crackers. Prick deeply with fork, and bake thoroughly.

WEIGHTS AND MEASURES.

4 liquid teaspoonfuls	equal	1 liquid tablespoonful
1	" tablespoonful	"	½ ounce
1	" pint	"	1 pound
2	" gills	"	1 cupful
1 kitchen cup		"	½ pint
4 cups of flour		"	1 pound
2 cups granul'td sugar	"	1 pound
3 cups corn-meal		"	1 pound
2 cups butter		"	1 pound
Butter size of an egg	"	2 ounces
1 tablespoonful butter	"	1 ounce
10 eggs		"	1 pound

CAKE.

GENERAL REMARKS.

Remember that different brands of flour vary in the amount of moisture required, so you may need to change the quantity of flour given in the receipts. If your cake cracks in the centre, you have made it too stiff.

You can always substitute for one teaspoonful of baking powder, one of cream of tartar and a half teaspoonful of soda. Most cakes require a moderate oven, especially true of the richer cakes.

☞ *Use SMITH'S COMMON SENSE Baking Powder and True-Fruit Flavoring Extracts. They are the best. See page 5.*

GINGER DROP CAKES.

One cupful of molasses, one of sour cream, one of brown sugar, two-thirds of a cupful of shortening, four cupfuls of flour, two eggs, one small dessert spoon of soda, one of ginger. Just before baking, grate in a little fresh orange peel, it gives a delicious flavor. Drop in small tins, bake in moderate oven.

MRS. SERVOSS.

MOLASSES CAKES.

One coffee cup of molasses, one of brown sugar, one teacup of butter, three eggs, two tablespoons of water and three teaspoons of soda, spices, flour to make soft dough. Roll thick, cut in cakes, bake in moderate oven.

MRS. A. S. MONTGOMERY.

GINGER DROPS.

One cup each of molasses and brown sugar, boiled with three-eighths cup of lard. When cool, add one teaspoon of soda, dissolved in one tablespoon of hot water, two well beaten eggs, two teaspoons of ginger, one of cinnamon; roll thin.

MRS. H. C. WILLIAMS.

GINGER COOKIES.

One cupful of butter, one of brown sugar, cream together, and add three beaten eggs, three even teaspoonfuls of soda, dissolved in hot water, two teaspoonfuls of ginger, a pinch of salt, and flour to make a soft dough.

MRS. SINCLAIR.

MOLASSES COOKIES.

Put in a coffee cup one teaspoon of ginger and one of soda; add a tablespoonful of boiling water, four tablespoonfuls of melted lard, and fill the cup with molasses. Stir until it foams, add flour enough to roll as soft as it can be handled.

CATHERINE COAPMAN.

CREAM COOKIES.

Two cups of sugar, one of rich sour cream, one-half cup of butter or shortening (with city cream, use three-fourths cupful),

☞ *Use SMITH'S COMMON SENSE Baking Powder and True-Fruit Flavoring Extracts. They are the best. See page 5.*

two eggs, two teaspoonfuls of baking powder, one of soda added to the cream. Do not make too stiff a dough.

Ora B. Fry.

SUGAR COOKIES.

One cupful of sugar, one-half cupful each of butter and sweet milk, one even teaspoonful of soda, three well beaten eggs, two heaping teaspoonfuls of baking powder, three cupfuls of flour.

Mrs. A. Elwood.

SCOTCH CAKES.

Two cupfuls of sugar, one cupful of butter, three eggs, one-fourth cup of milk, one-fourth teaspoonful of soda, flour enough to rool. After cutting the cakes, dip their tops in a dish containing one teaspoonful of cinnamon and one cup of brown sugar mixed. Bake in good oven.

Mrs. W. P. Bigelow.

SOFT GINGERBREAD.

Beat together the yolks of three eggs and one-half cupful of lard, add one-half cupful of milk, one and one-half cupfuls of New Orleans molasses, one teaspoonful of soda, one tablespoonful of ginger, and three cupfuls of flour. Beat the whites of the eggs stiff and add last. Bake in moderate oven three-quarters of an hour.

Mrs. Makeham.

WATER CAKE.

One egg, one cupful of molasses, one tablespoonful of butter, one teaspoonful of ginger, three tablespoonfuls of water, one teaspoonful of soda, two cupfuls of flour.

Mrs. Almstead.

JUMBLES.

Two cups of sugar, one of butter creamed together, three eggs well beaten, one-half teaspoonful of soda, dissolved in one-fourth cup of sweet milk, four cups of flour.

Mrs. Sinclair.

☞ *Use SMITH'S COMMON SENSE Baking Powder and True-Fruit Flavoring Extracts. They are the best. See page 5.*

FRUIT JUMBLES.

One cupful of sugar, one-fourth cupful of butter, two eggs, one-half cupful of milk, three even spoonfuls of baking powder, one-half cupful of currants, and two scant cupfuls of flour.

C. E.

CREAM PUFFS.

To one teacup of boiling water, add one-half cup of butter; when it boils, add a bit of soda the size of a pea, and one cup of flour, and stir until smooth, boiling constantly. When cool, but not cold, add the eggs, well beaten, and stir all together, until very light and smooth. Take a teaspoonful of the dough for a puff and drop on a buttered tin, spreading it a little. Place puffs far enough apart so that they will not run together. Bake twenty-five minutes in an oven hot enough for biscuit. When cold, fill through a small opening in the side.

CREAM FOR FILLING.—One cup of milk, one-half cup of sugar, three tablespoons of flour, one egg; boil like any custard; flavor to taste.

MRS. C. H. WHEELER.

PORK CAKE.

One cupful of molasses and one-half teaspoonful of soda, dissolved in boiling water; add one cup of milk, one of finely chopped fat pork, and four of flour; add last one cup of finely chopped raisins. Bake in slow oven one hour.

MRS. MAKEHAM.

COFFEE CAKE.

One cup of sugar, one-half cup each of butter and strong coffee, one cup each of currants and seeded raisins, one-half cup of citron, two eggs, one large teaspoonful of baking powder, spice to taste. Bake in slow oven.

MRS. BABBAGE.

COFFEE CAKE.

One cupful, each of butter, brown sugar, molasses, and *strong*, cold coffee; two eggs, two teaspoons of soda, spice, three and one-half cups of flour.

MRS. JAMES ALDRICH.

☞ Use *SMITH'S COMMON SENSE Baking Powder and True-Fruit Flavoring Extracts. They are the best. See page 5.*

DELICATE CAKE.

Cream two cups of sugar and one-half cup of butter; add three-quarters of a cupful of sweet milk and the whites of six eggs, then three cupfuls of flour and three spoonfuls of baking powder.

Mrs. S. C. VanHoesen.

GOLD CAKE.

Cream two cups of sugar and one-half of butter, add the beaten yolks of four eggs, one cup of water, three of flour and two teaspoons of baking powder.

Mrs. H. J. Beers.

PLAIN CAKE.

One cup of sugar, one good tablespoonful of butter, one egg, two-thirds cup of milk, two teaspoonfuls of baking powder, one and one-half cups of flour. Flavor to suit. Sprinkle with a little granulated sugar before putting in the oven.

Mrs. S. C. Van Hoesen.

GRAHAM CAKE.

One-half cup each of sugar and molasses, one cup of sour milk and one even tablespoonful of soda dissolved in it. To this, add four tablespoonfuls of melted butter, two cups of Graham flour and one cup of currants.

Mrs. H. G. Beers.

BREAD CAKE.

Four cupfuls of raised dough, one of butter, two of sugar, one of raisins, two eggs, one teaspoonful of soda, cinnamon and nutmeg to taste.

Ora B. Fry.

SPICE CAKE.

One cupful of brown sugar, one of molasses, one of sour milk, in which is dissolved one heaping teaspoon of soda, three-fourths cupful of butter, spices to taste, three and one-half cups of flour (scant), one cupful each of raisins and currants, dredged with flour, and three eggs.

Ora B. Fry.

☞ Use SMITH'S COMMON SENSE Baking Powder and True-Fruit Flavoring Extracts. They are the best. See page 5.

SPONGE CAKE.

Beat the yolks of three eggs, add one and one-half cups of sugar, beat very light, then one-half cup of boiling water and two cups of sifted flour mixed with two teaspoonfuls of baking powder; lastly the whites beaten stiff.

MRS. A. FOULDS.

DELICATE SPONGE CAKE.

One pound of sugar, one half pound of flour and ten eggs. Beat the sugar and yolks to a foam, the whites to a stiff froth, add lemon to the sugar and yolks to flavor, then flour, then whites. It takes two persons to make it quickly and properly.

MRS. SINCLAIR.

SPONGE CREAM CAKE.

Beat three eggs very light, add one teacup of very dry A coffee sugar and a pinch of salt, then three tablespoonfuls of water, and last one teacup of flour, measured before sifted, and two full teaspoonfuls of baking powder. Bake in two layers. Fill with a cream made of one cup of milk, thickened and sweetened to taste, to which the yolk of one egg is added just as it is taken from the fire. Frost the top with the whites.

MRS. MILLER.

ICE CREAM CAKE.

Two cups of powdered sugar, one of cornstarch, two of flour, three-fourths cup of butter, whites of seven eggs beaten stiff, one teaspoon of baking powder, cream, butter and sugar; add beaten whites, then sift in flour and corn-starch. Put together with boiled icing.

MRS. BEIRS.

CHOCOLATE CAKE.

Mix one-half cake of Baker's chocolate grated, one-half cup of sweet milk, one cup of sugar, yolk of one egg, one teaspoonful of vanilla; boil until smooth. Beat this mixture into a cake batter made as follows: One cup of sugar creamed with one-half cup of butter, add one-half cup of sweet milk, two eggs, yolks and whites beaten separately, one teaspoon of soda, two and one-half cups of flour. Bake, frost with white icing.

MRS. GEO. HERR.

☞ *Use SMITH'S COMMON SENSE Baking Powder and True-Fruit Flavoring Extracts. They are the best. See page 5.*

NUT CAKE.

Cream two cupfuls of sugar very light with one-third cupful of butter, add the beaten whites and yolks of four eggs, and one cup of sweet milk and three cups of flour sifted, with three even teaspoonfuls of baking powder. Just before putting in the oven, add one cupful of finely chopped nut meats dredged with flour. Bake in large square tin in moderate oven. Frost with either boiled or confectioner's icing, and place walnut meats on the icing so as to cut in square pieces with a nut on each piece.

MRS. D. A. WOODBURY.

WALNUT CAKE.

One coffeecupful of sugar, one-half of butter, one-half of sweet milk, three eggs, beaten separately, two and one-half cupfuls of flour, two teaspoonfuls of baking powder, two cupfuls of raisins, stoned and cut, and one of walnut meats chopped slightly.

MRS. S. R. TAYLOR.

WHITE CAKE—RELIABLE.

One cup of sugar, one-half cup each of butter and milk, one and one-fourth cups of flour, one-fourth cup of corn starch, two level spoonfuls of baking powder, whites of three and one-half eggs. Cream sugar and butter, add milk slowly, then flour, corn-starch, baking powder and beaten whites.

The yolks with one egg added, and then the same recipe followed, will make a delicious gold cake. These two recipes may be used as foundations for all kinds of layer cake.

MRS. GRORGE WETMORE.

MARTHA'S CAKE.

Three eggs, one cup of sugar, butter the size of an egg, one cup of, flour, one teaspoonful of cream of tartar sifted in the flour, one-half teaspoonful of soda, dissolved in a tablespoonful of milk. Bake in jelly cake tins and spread when cold with fruit jelly. This cake seldom fails, and when well mixed and baked, is very nice.

MISS M. PEARCE.

☞ *Use SMITH'S COMMON SENSE Baking Powder and True-Fruit Flavoring Extracts. They are the best. See page 5.*

FRENCH CAKE.

Half cup of butter, three eggs, two cups of sugar, three cups of flour, one cup of milk, two teaspoons of cream of tartar and one teaspoon of soda. Beat the yolks of the eggs in the milk, add the butter and the sugar, then the flour and the cream of tartar, then the whites of the eggs, and last of all, the soda. Whip the whites of the eggs before adding them to the cake, and dissolve the soda in a little milk or water. This receipt may be used either as a sponge or layer cake with equal success.

MISS PEARCE.

CUSTARD CAKE.

Two eggs, beaten separately, one cupful of sugar, one tablespoonful of butter, four tablespoonfuls of cold water, one cupful of flour and one heaping teaspoonful of baking powder. Bake in three layers and put together with a cream made as follows: One-half cupful of sugar, three-fourths cupful of milk and one tablespoonful of corn-starch; boil until as thick as jelly, and flavor to taste.

MISS S. R. TAYLOR.

ALMOND CREAM CAKE.

Two cups of sugar (pulverized), one-fourth cup of butter, one cup of sweet milk, three cups of flour, three teaspoons of baking powder, whites of four eggs, beaten very light, and one-half teaspoonful of vanilla. Bake in four layers.

CREAM—Whip one cupful of sweet cream to a froth, stir gradually into it one-half cupful of pulverized sugar, a few drops of vanilla, and one pound of almonds, blanched and chopped. Spread quite thickly between the layers and frost the top and sides. Scald the nuts after shelling and the brown skins will come off easily.

ALICE LOUGHBOROUGH.

SUPERIOR SUNSHINE CAKE.

Take whites of seven eggs, yolks of five, one cup of granulated sugar, two-thirds cup of flour, one-third teaspoon of cream of tartar; add a pinch of salt. Sift, measure, and set aside flour and sugar. Beat the yolks of eggs thoroughly, the whites about

---

Use SMITH'S COMMON SENSE Baking Powder and True-Fruit Flavoring Extracts. They are the best. See page 5.

half; add cream of tartar and beat very thoroughly. Stir in sugar, then the beaten yolks, add flour, and flavor to taste. Put in a tube-pan and into the oven at once. Should bake in thirty-five to fifty minutes. Use pastry flour.

Mrs. J. W. Johnson.

PORTSMOUTH ORANGE CAKE.

Grate the rind of an orange, squeeze over it the juice of half an orange, and add one teaspoonful of tartaric acid; stand aside for one-half hour. Meanwhile mix a teaspoonful of baking powder with one cup of sifted flour; sift three times and set aside. Separate the whites and yolks of four large eggs; to the yolks add one cup of granulated sugar, and beat very light; add the juice and grated rind of half a lemon; beat again; last, add the flour with baking powder and the whites beaten stiff. Bake in two layers.

Icing—Add a cupful of confectioner's sugar to the orange juice, already prepared; stir thoroughly and it is done. If too stiff, add more orange juice; if too thin, more sugar. Put between the cakes a filling of sweet oranges sliced thin; cover with this icing, and the cake will be ready to serve in an hour or two. It is better eaten soon after icing it.

Mrs. S. E. Barrett.

ORANGE ROLL.

Four eggs, white and yolks beaten separately, one-half pint of powdered sugar, one-half pint of sifted flour, two tablespoonfuls of boiling water, one teaspoonful of baking powder. Bake in a sheet ten minutes in a quick oven; spread with orange marmalade and roll.

JELLY ROLL.

Beat separately the yolks and whites of three eggs; to them add one even teacupful of sugar, one-half egg shell of water, one even teacupful of flour, and two even teaspoons of baking powder. Bake in a square shallow tin in a moderate oven. Turn on a towel, bottom side up, spread with jelly roll, and

---

☞ *Use SMITH'S COMMON SENSE Baking Powder and True-Fruit Flavoring Extracts. They are the best. See page 5.*

leave it wrapped in the towel. Four eggs may be used, and the water omitted. Be sure that the measuring cup is a teacup and not a larger size. MRS. HENRY BEIGLER.

FRUIT CAKE WITHOUT EGGS.

One pound of fat pork, chopped fine; pour over it one pint of boiling water or coffee, two cups of molasses, one of sugar, one and one-half pounds of raisins, one-half pound of currants, spice, one teaspoonful of soda, eight cups of flour.

MRS. H. DOTY.

CONFECTIONERY CAKE.

One coffeecup of sugar, three-fourths coffeecup butter, two of flour, one of milk, whites of five eggs, three teaspoons baking powder. To one tablespoonful of this cake, add one-half cup each of chopped raisins, citron, flour and molasses, and spice to taste. Bake in three layers, two white and one dark. Put together with soft frosting. MRS. HURD.

FRUIT CAKE.

One pound of flour, one of brown sugar, one cupful of molasses, three-fourths pound of butter, eight eggs, one pound of citron, one pound of raisins, spice to taste. Cream butter and sugar, beats yolks and whites separately, add molasses, flour, fruit. Bake two hours. MRS. ALMSTEAD.

FRUIT CAKE.

Four eggs, one cupful each of butter, molasses, strong coffee, two of brown sugar, four of flour, one pound each of raisins and currants, one-half pound of citron, one teaspoonful of soda, one of cloves, two of cinnamon, one whole nutmeg.

MISS HATTIE SKINNER.

MOCHA CAKE.

Cream together one-half cup of butter with one of sugar; add one-half cup of corn starch mixed with one-half cup of milk, then one and one-quarter cups of flour, into which is sifted one-

---

☞ *Use SMITH'S COMMON SENSE Baking Powder and True-Fruit Flavoring Extracts. They are the best. See page 5.*

half teaspoonful of soda and one of cream-tartar; last add the beaten whites of three eggs. Bake in two layers.

MOCHA CREAM FOR FILLING.—Put four large tablespoonfuls of Mocha coffee, ground to a powder, in a French coffee pot. Pour over it slowly one-half cup boiling water; repeat this twice. (If without a French coffee pot, the coffee may be filtered through a little bag made of strong thick cotton or drilling.) Reserve three tablespoonfuls of this liquid coffee for the icing, and add to the remainder three-fourths cupful of milk, scant. Put in a double boiler, and when it boils, stir into it two tablespoonfuls of flour (or one of corn starch), beaten with the white of one and yolks of four eggs and one cup of sugar. Cook until smooth, stirring constantly. When this cream is lukewarm, beat into it two tablespoonfuls of butter, and spread upon one of the cakes, placing the other over it. Ice the top thickly with soft frosting mixed with the three tablespoonfuls of coffee reserved.

MISS S. E. BARRETT.

NEAPOLITAN CAKE.

Make a recipe as for Mocha cake, and into half of it stir liquid cochineal, drop by drop, until a light pink; bake in two layers, one white and one pink. Prepare the cochineal by boiling one-half ounce of pure cochineal, one tablespoonful each of sugar and cream-tartar, and a piece of alum the size of a pea, in one-half cup of water for fifteen minutes. Strain and bottle, and use for coloring cake, jellies and cream, as it is perfectly harmless. For the other two layers, make a cake as before, substituting the yolks of the eggs with one egg additional. Bake half of it, and to the remainder add one ounce of Baker's chocolate, three tablespoonfuls of sugar and one taplespoonful of water, melted over the fire. Put the four layers together with a soft frosting, flavored with orange juice.

MISS S. E. BARRETT.

CHOCOLATE ICINGS.

I. One-fourth cake Baker's chocolate, one cup of sugar, three-fourths cup of milk, scant. Boil together until perfectly smooth and thickened somewhat. Flavor, and when *nearly* cold, spread on the cake.

☞ Use *SMITH'S COMMON SENSE Baking Powder and True-Fruit Flavoring Extracts. They are the best. See page 5.*

II. One cupful of sugar, seven teaspoonfuls of water; boil until it will string when dropped from a spoon. Stir this hot syrup gradually over the beaten white of one egg, white still warm, add seven tablespoonfuls of grated chocolate, and one teaspoonful of vanilla.

ANGEL FOOD.

Add one even teaspoonful of cream-tartar to one even cupful of flour; sift together three times. Have ready one and one-half cupfuls of granulated sugar. Beat the whites of eleven eggs very, very stiff, whip into them lightly the sugar, then the sifted flour, and bake in ungreased tins kept for this cake alone. The usual shape is round with a tube in the centre, reaching higher than the sides of the pan. This recipe will fill two of the medium sized, or one large sized pan of this style. Bake forty or fifty minutes in a slow oven; when done, turn the pan over so that it rests on the tube, and after an hour the cake will easily loosen and slide out of the pan. Ice the bottom and sides with confectioner's icing.

Mrs. W. A. Montgomery.

CONFECTIONER'S ICING.

Use the confectioner's sugar and moisten it with water or milk; beat until thick and creamy, flavor as desired, spread on the cake and it will dry in an hour. Very little liquid is required to moisten the sugar; it should be added cautiously, little by little.

PIES AND PUDDINGS.

To make good pastry, observe the following directions:

Have all the ingredients *cold*.

Do not mix the flour and shortening to a powder, but allow the shortening to remain in small flakes.

☞ Use *SMITH'S COMMON SENSE Baking Powder and True-Fruit Flavoring Extracts. They are the best. See page 5.*

Add only enough water to make a crumbly dough, and add it so gradually that no portion is made pasty.

Have the oven hot the first ten minutes, cooler after that.

PLAIN PIE CRUST.

To one quart of sifted flour take one half cupful each of lard and butter and a pinch of salt, mix lightly, add gradually about three-fourths of a cupful of ice water, and roll thin, using as little flour as possible. This may also be made with lard or butter alone. M.

SUET CRUST.

Chop very fine one-half pound of beef suet, add to it three cupfuls of sifted flour and a teaspoonful of salt, mix, and add about one cupful of ice water. M.

POTATO CRUST.

Add to a cupful of hot mashed potato a half cupful of cream or milk, and beat very light with an egg beater; add enough flour to make a soft dough, and roll out. Many use an even spoonful of baking powder mixed with the flour. Good for meat pies.

PUFF PASTE.

Mix a piece of butter the size of an egg thoroughly into one even pint of flour, add ice water enough to make a hard dough. Roll out this dough on the board, and cover the top thickly with bits of butter, then roll up the dough tightly like a jelly roll. Cut this roll in three pieces and put them on top of each other, *the cut ends at the sides, never on top.* Press down with the rolling pin and roll out again, always rolling the same way, so as to keep the layers undisturbed. Cover with bits of butter, roll up tightly and proceed exactly as before. After covering with the bits of butter for the third time, rolling up and cutting, the paste should be set on the ice until very cold before using. It may be wrapped in a cloth, and kept for a week on ice. When you wish to use it, press the rolls flat, and roll as before, keeping the layers right. It may be rolled very thin as it will puff up in the oven to many times its original thickness. All bits left should be laid flat on each other, and not molded into a lump.

☞ Use *SMITH'S COMMON SENSE Baking Powder and True-Fruit Flavoring Extracts. They are the best. See page* 5.

as that spoils the grain. The paste must be icy cold when put in the oven, and the oven very hot. Many cooks wash the butter used in making puff pastry until elastic and waxy. B.

LEMON PIE.

Bake a shell of rich pie crust, pricking it carefully to avoid air bubbles. Have ready a filling made of one cupful each of water and sugar, into which, when boiling hot, is stirred the juice and grated rind of one large or two small lemons, two tablespoonfuls of corn starch, and last, when this mixture has cooked clear, the beaten yolks of two eggs. Place this when cold in the shell, cover with a meringue made of the whites, and brown for a moment in the oven. The amount of corn starch may need to be increased a little with very juicy lemons; flour may be used instead, but does not make so clear or pleasing a jelly. One egg may be used instead of two.
Mrs. A. J. Barrett.

LEMON PIE.

The juice and grated rind of one lemon, one egg, one cup of sugar, three crackers rolled *fine*, one teaspoonful of butter, one cup of boiling water. This is for one pie.
Mrs. James Aldrich.

MOCK MINCE PIE.

Three milk crackers rolled, one cupful of cold water, one of molasses, one-half of sugar, one-half of vinegar, one-half each of raisins and currants, one beaten egg, two tablespoonfuls of butter, cinnamon, cloves and nutmeg to taste, five apples chopped fine. Mix all together and bake as mince pie. This recipe makes two pies. Mrs. Babbage.

[Other recipes omit the apple and substitute bread crumbs for crackers.—Ed.]

MINCE PIE.

Two pounds of meat, four pounds of apples, three pounds of sugar, one pound of raisins, one-half pint of boiled cider, one tablespoon of cloves, three tablespoons of cinnamon, three tablespoons of allspice, one tablespoon of nutmeg, one cup molasses. Mix together, heat scalding hot and put in jar.
Miss Skinner.

☞ *Use SMITH'S COMMON SENSE Baking Powder and True-Fruit Flavoring Extracts. They are the best. See page 5.*

CHOICE STRAWBERRY PIE.

Take three cups of strawberries, one cup of sugar. Line pie plate with crust, pricked over with fork to prevent blistering or shrinking; cut top crust out a little larger than the bottom one, prick also and bake. Put the fruit and sugar in the pie plate and cover with the top crust. If the fruit be ripe, they will steam tender; if not, return to oven until heated through.

Mrs. J. W. Johnson.

CRANBERRY PIE.

Fill a pie tin with uncooked cranberries, add one large cupful of sugar, cover with upper crust and bake. The cranberries should be washed so that they will be damp, and the sugar sprinkled with water. Stewed cranberries may be used if preferred.

CHERRY AND BERRY PIES.

Dredge the fruit with flour to prevent the juice from being watery. Press the edges of the pies very closely together. A narrow strip of cotton cloth, dampened and pressed firmly over the two edges of a juicy pie will hold them together and prevent the juice running out. When the pie is baked, the strip may be easily pulled off without injury.

CREAM PIE.

Scald one pint of milk, add one-half cupful of sugar, two heaping tablespoonfuls of corn starch, and last, the yolks of two eggs. Flavor with almond, orange, vanilla, or lemon. When cold, fill a pastry shell with this cream, make a meringue of the whites of the eggs and brown delicately. A cupful of fresh cocoanut will make this delicious.

GERMAN APPLE PIE.

Take a deep pudding dish holding two quarts, and in the center invert a tea cup. Fill this dish with sliced apples, sweeten with a little sugar, sprinkle with cinnamon, and pour over it one cupful of water. Cover the top with a biscuit crust, made with one pint of flour, one tablespoonful of butter, two teaspoonfuls of baking powder, and milk enough to make a soft

---

☞ *Use SMITH'S COMMON SENSE Baking Powder and True-Fruit Flavoring Extracts. They are the best. See page 5.*

dough. Bake in a moderate oven. Upon opening, the inverted cup will be found full of delicious juice. Any fruit pie is wholesome baked thus, without under crust. They may be served with or without additional sauce. Are very good with sugar and cream.   MRS. S.

CHOCOLATE PIE.

One coffee cup of milk, two heaping tablespoonfuls of grated chocolate, three-fourths teacup of sugar, yolks of three eggs. Heat chocolate and milk together, add sugar and yolks together, beaten to cream. Flavor with vanilla. Bake with under crust. Spread meringue of whites over the top, and brown slightly.

MRS. C. H. WHEELER.

HOT PUDDINGS.

PLUM PUDDING.
(John Bull's Own.)

One pound of suet, one pound of moist sugar, one pound of mixed candied peel, one-half pound bread crumbs, one-half pound flour, eight eggs, one pound of currants, one pound of raisins, one pound of sultana raisins, one teaspoonful of salt, one teaspoonful of mixed spice. Chop the suet fine, stone the raisins, wash and dry the currants, chop the peel, and sift the bread crumbs. Mix in the following order; flour, salt, spices, sugar, raisins, peel, bread crumbs, sultanas, and currants. Beat the eggs, and strain them for ten minutes; pour over the mass; stir for twenty-five minutes. Butter a mould and fill it, scald a clean cloth and flour it, tie the pudding down and boil for thirteen hours.

MRS. T. HARWOOD PATTISON.

SUET PUDDING.

One cupful of suet chopped, one cupful of raisins stoned, one cupful of sweet milk, two and one-half cupfuls of flour, one-third

---

☞ *Use SMITH'S COMMON SENSE Baking Powder and True-Fruit Flavoring Extracts. They are the best. See page 5.*

cupful of dark molasses, two even teaspoonfuls of baking powder, a little spice, i. e. cloves, nutmeg and cinnamon, raisins, chopped in one-half cup of flour. Steam three hours.

MRS. ALDRICH.

STEAMED PUDDING.

Two-thirds of a cupful of sugar, one cupful of sweet milk, three of flour, two tablespoonfuls of butter, two teaspoonfuls of baking powder, yolks of two eggs. Steam one hour in buttered dish.

SAUCE.

To one cupful of boiling water, add one heaping tablespoonful of corn starch, and boil until clear. When cold, whip this starch gradually into one cupful of sugar, and one-half cupful of butter, which have been already creamed. When perfectly smooth and velvety, add the whites of two eggs beaten stiff, and any flavoring desired. [This is a delicious sauce. Ed.]

MRS. A. FOULDS.

VICTORIA PUDDING.

One-half pound of carrots and potatoes grated raw, one-half pound each of suet, flour, and currants, one-fourth pound of raisins, one-half cupful of molasses, one tablespoonful of brown sugar, soda, spice. Steam four hours.

MRS. A. ELWOOD.

GRAHAM PUDDING.

To one cupful each of milk and molasses, add one beaten egg, two and one-half cupfuls of graham flour, two teaspoonfuls of baking powder, one cupful of raisins, salt, spice to taste. Steam three hours.

MISS KITTIE HEACOCK.

PUFF PUDDING.

Into two and one-half tablespoonfuls of flour mixed with one-half teaspoonful of baking powder, stir gradually one cupful of milk; then add the beaten yolks of three eggs, a pinch of salt, and last, the whites beaten stiff. Bake one-half hour. Serve with hot sauce.

MRS. J. W. BROOKS.

☞ *Use SMITH'S COMMON SENSE Baking Powder and True-Fruit Flavoring Extracts. They are the best. See page 5.*

PUDDING.

Stir into a quart of scalding milk six tablespoonfuls of sugar, three of corn starch. Add the beaten yolks of five eggs; remove from the fire, flavor, then bake fifteen minutes. Make a meringue for the top, of the whites of eggs, and three tablespoonfuls of powdered sugar; brown in the oven. Serve hot or cold.

Mrs. Beers.

RAISIN PUFFS.

Two eggs, one-half cup butter, three teaspoonfuls baking powder, two tablespoonfuls sugar, two cups of flour, one cup of milk, and one of raisins chopped fine. Steam one-half hour in small cups.

Mrs. C. E. Meade.

HANNAH WHIPPLE'S PUDDING.

Four cupfuls fine pieces of bread or cake, measured before soaking, one cupful (good measure) sweet milk, one-half cupful molasses, one cupful stoned raisins, one-half cupful melted butter, one teaspoonful soda, a little chopped citron, spice of several kinds, to taste. The milk should be poured over the bread and left for a while to soak. Then add the other ingredients, the fruit slightly floured, the soda dissolved in a little *cold* water, and put the whole into a well buttered mould, allowing plenty of room to rise. Boil three hours without stopping.

Mrs. C. E. Meade.

INDIAN MEAL PUDDING.

Put three pints of milk in a kettle; when boiling, add ten even tablespoonfuls of fine corn meal wet with a little cold milk, stirring carefully to avoid lumps. When partly cold, two-thirds coffeecupful of molasses, one-half pint of milk, cinnamon and salt to taste. Bake for three hours in a well buttered pudding dish. When half done, pour over it a half pint of cold milk.

Mrs. C. H. Wheeler.

TAPIOCA PUDDING.

Put two tablespoonfuls of pearl tapioca in one pint of milk, cold, and add one tablespoonful of butter. Place over the fire until it thickens or boils, remove from the stove, add one pint

☞ Use *SMITH'S COMMON SENSE Baking Powder* and *True-Fruit Flavoring Extracts*. They are the best. *See page 5.*

of milk, and sugar to taste. When quite cold, add two well beaten eggs, and bake one-half hour in moderate oven. To be eaten either hot or cold.

Mrs. S. C. Van Hoesen.

GOLDEN PUDDING.

Cream four even teaspoonfuls of butter with one cupful of powdered sugar and the yolks of three eggs. Add one teacupful of corn meal, and three whites beaten stiff. Bake in a moderate oven one-half hour. Serve with the sauce given under "Steamed Pudding," or, if preferred, any hot sauce. Delicious.

Miss S. E. Barrett.

WONDERFUL PUDDING.

Put one-half cupful of uncooked rice in a pudding dish, pour over it five cupfuls of sweet milk slightly sweetened ; bake three hours in a *slow* oven, stirring occasionally. To be eaten hot or cold ; if hot, with foam sauce ; if cold, with cream and sugar. This pudding is delicious if well cooked; it should be a smooth cream. If the oven is too hot, it may be allowed to simmer on the back of the stove until nearly done, then the cover removed and the pudding browned in the oven. Serve with the following:

FOAM SAUCE.

Beat the yolks of two eggs light, cream with them one cupful of powdered sugar, stand the bowl containing them in boiling water, and stir occasionally until the mixture is warm throughout. Then add the whites beaten stiff, and one tablespoonful of boiling water just before serving. Flavor as desired.

Mrs. A. J. Barrett.

CABINET PUDDING.

Butter a bowl or pudding mould, and fill with layers of stale bread or cake crumbs, sprinkled with raisins. Pour over this enough sweetened milk and egg to just cover the bread or cake.

The quantity of milk must be determined by the size of the mould ; a quart mould will take about three cupfuls of milk. Allow one egg for each cupful of milk used. When the mould is filled, allow it to stand about fifteen minutes, then place it in

---

☞ *Use SMITH'S COMMON SENSE Baking Powder and True-Fruit Flavoring Extracts. They are the best. See page 5.*

a pot of boiling water, and boil steadily for one hour. Turn out of the mould, and serve with hot sauce or fairy butter.

M.

ROLY POLY.

Roll a good baking powder crust about one inch thick, spread with fruit jam, roll it up, and tie up in well floured cloth, leaving room to swell. Steam two hours. Serve with foam sauce.

APPLE DUMPLINGS.

Make a crust with one quart of flour, one large tablespoonful of lard or butter, three teaspoonfuls of baking powder, and about one cupful of milk, using more or less as the flour requires to make a good biscuit dough. Roll out the dough half an inch in thickness, cut it out with large cutter about the size of a saucer. Have ready the apples pared and cored, place one apple on each piece of dough, fill the center of the apple with sugar (if desired), and work the dough up to cover the apple. Set the dumplings on a large greased plate, put in a steamer, and steam thirty to forty minutes according to the apples. Serve with maple sugar and butter, hard sauce, or sugar and cream.

MRS. A. S. MONTGOMERY.

COTTAGE PUDDING.

One cup of flour, one tablespoonful of butter, one-half cup of sugar, one egg, one-third cup sweet milk, one heaping teaspoon baking powder. Bake in round tin or dish, and serve with sauce.

MRS. BEERS.

FIG PUDDING.

One-half pound each of finely chopped figs, suet and bread, one-half pound of brown sugar, two eggs, a pinch of salt. Steam three hours. Serve with foam sauce.

MRS. WILLIS UPTON.

RAISIN PUFFS.

Two eggs, one-fourth cupful of butter, two cupfuls of flour, one of milk, one of raisins chopped fine, three teaspoonfuls of

---

☞ *Use SMITH'S COMMON SENSE Baking Powder and True-Fruit Flavoring Extracts. They are the best. See page 5.*

baking powder. Steam one-half hour in buttered cups, turn out and serve with hot sweet sauce.

Mrs. A. Elwood.

BOSTON STRAWBERRY SHORTCAKE.

One-half cup of sugar creamed with one tablespoonful of butter, and one beaten egg, one-third cup of milk, one cup of flour, and one heaping teaspoon of baking powder. Bake in two thin layers. Take a quart of sweet berries, slice them, but do not mash or bruise. Stir over them lightly one pint of thick whipped cream, well sweetened; place a layer several inches thick of berries and cream between the cakes, and serve immediately. Be sure that you do not crush the berries in any way to extract the juice, or they will render the cream thin. Mix the berries and cream the last thing before serving. The upper crust may be heaped with whipped cream if desired.

Mrs. W. A. Montgomery.

STRAWBERRY SHORTCAKE.

Crust: one quart of flour, one-half cupful of butter, three teaspoonfuls of baking powder, and milk to make a soft dough. Steam or bake in large square tin. Filling: mash three pints of strawberries, sweeten partially; then add one cupful of sugar beaten to a cream with one-half cupful of butter. Pour this filling over and around the shortcake and serve immediately.

Mrs. Servoss.

APPLE SHORTCAKE.

Make crust as above, and roll it out in two large layers, butter each of them, and lay them buttered sides together in a square tin. Bake, remove the upper layer, and fill with well seasoned apple sauce. Put on the top layer, cover it with whipped cream, and serve. [Stewed Apricots or Prunes are delicious served in this same way. Ed.]

Mrs. Servoss.

ORANGE SHORTCAKE.

One egg, one cup of milk, two tablespoonfuls of butter, two cups of flour, two teaspoonfuls of baking powder; baked in two

☞ *Use SMITH'S COMMON SENSE Baking Powder and True-Fruit Flavoring Extracts. They are the best. See page 5.*

shallow tins. One-half dozen oranges sliced ; cover with sugar. Pour the oranges between and over the cake.

Mrs. Wm. A. Cogswell.

PUFF PUDDING.

Put two teaspoons of baking powder and a little salt into a pint of flour, and mix very soft with milk. Grease cups. Put one spoonful of batter into the bottom of the cup, and then a spoonful of any kind of canned fruit (cherries are best), and a spoonful of batter on top. Steam twenty minutes, and eat with sauce.

Mrs. Koehler.

BROWN BETTY.

A layer of bread crumbs in the bottom of a pudding dish, then one of apples, and so on, having the last layer crumbs. Pour over one-half cupful each of molasses and water mixed, and bake in a moderate oven. If molasses is not liked, a pleasing variety in this pudding is produced by using slices of buttered bread, slightly sprinkled with cold water in the layers, alternating with apple. Over the top layer of apples, sprinkle fine crumbs, those used for croquettes, and bake.

H. B.

PUDDING SAUCES.

CREAMY SAUCE.

Cream together one-half cup each of butter and powdered sugar, beating until very light. Add, little by little, three tablespoonfuls of thick, sweet cream. Place the bowl in boiling water, and stir until the sauce is heated a very few moments. Flavor and serve.

FAIRY BUTTER.

Cream together one heaping teaspoonful of butter, and one cupful of powdered sugar, add the white of one egg unbeaten,

---

☞ *Use SMITH'S COMMON SENSE Baking Powder and True-Fruit Flavoring Extracts. They are the best. See page 5.*

and beat until frothy, then the white of one egg beaten stiff, and one teaspoonful of vanilla. Mix lightly, and heap on a small dish ; set on the ice to harden.

FOAM SAUCE.

One and one-half cupfuls of boiling water, one of sugar, one dessert spoonful of corn starch, butter the size of an egg. When boiled clear, add the juice of half a lemon, and, while boiling hot, pour, just before serving, into a sauce dish in which you have placed one-half teaspoonful of soda. Stir and it will foam.

MRS. BIGELOW.

ALMOND PUDDING SAUCE.

Beat one egg and one cupful of powdered sugar to a froth, add one-half teaspoonful of almond extract, and just before serving, six tablespoonfuls of boiling milk.

G. A.

PUDDING SAUCE.

Beat the yolks of two eggs and the white of one with a half-cup of sugar ; flavor. Over this pour one teacupful of *boiling* milk, gradually stirring all the time. Beat the other white stiff, and stir in lightly. A pretty and delicate sauce. Be sure to pour the boiling milk over the egg, and not the egg into the milk, as the egg and sugar must not actually boil.

N. E.

FRUIT PUDDING SAUCE.

One-half cup butter, two and one-half cups sugar, one dessert spoonful corn starch, wet in a little cold milk, juice of one lemon, and half the grated peel, one cup boiling water. Cream the butter and sugar well, pour the corn starch into the boiling water, and stir over a clear fire until well thickened ; put all together in a bowl and beat five minutes before returning to the saucepan. Heat once almost to the boiling point and serve.

MRS. C. E. MEADE.

☞ *Use SMITH'S COMMON SENSE Baking Powder and True-Fruit Flavoring Extracts. They are the best. See page 5.*

COLD PUDDINGS AND DESSERTS.

PRUNE PUDDING.

One pound of prunes boiled soft; drain and add one and one-half cups of granulated sugar, stir in the beaten whites of five eggs, and bake in a quick oven fifteen minutes. Serve with custard made of the yolks and one pint of milk.

Mrs. Frank Upton.

LEMON CREAM.

Grate the rind of two lemons and squeeze the juice. Beat the whites and yolks of six eggs separately. Mix the whites, lemons and one pint of water; stand aside one hour. Beat the yolks with one pint of sugar and one tablespoonful of corn starch; add to the whites and lemons. Boil like custard.

Mrs. James Aldrich.

ORANGE PUDDING.

Take four large oranges, peel, seed and cut into small pieces; sweeten to taste. Boil one pint of milk, sweeten, add to it one tablespoonful of corn starch, dissolved in a little cold milk, and the yolks of three eggs beaten. When thickened, cool and pour over the oranges. Beat the whites stiff, add one-half teacup of sugar; spread over the pudding and brown slightly. Eaten cold.

Mrs. C. H. Wheeler.

SEA FOAM PUDDING.

Make a lemon jelly and let it harden. Beat the white of one egg stiff; spread it over the jelly. Take the yolk of one egg, add half a cup of granulated sugar, a pinch of corn starch, and beat thoroughly. Scald a half pint of milk and pour it over the beaten yolk and sugar. Put over the fire and heat until it thickens; flavor to taste, cool and pour over the jelly when served.

Mrs. J. W. Johnson.

☞ Use *SMITH'S COMMON SENSE Baking Powder and True-Fruit Flavoring Extracts. They are the best. See page 5.*

RIBBON PUDDING.

Let one pint of new milk come to boiling point. Add one-half cup of sugar, and two tablespoonfuls each of grated chocolate and corn starch. Boil until thickened. Take same quanity of milk, sugar and corn starch as the above (leaving out the chocolate). Bring it to a boiling point. When both are done, have ready a deep dish, and put a layer of the dark pudding, then a layer of the light, doing this till all is used up. When cold, turn out, bottom side up, into a glass dish, and serve with sugar and cream. Flavor with vanilla.

S. R. TAYLOR.

CHOCOLATE PUDDING.

A half box of Cox's gelatine, one quart of milk and a quarter cake of Baker's chocolate. Pour half the milk upon the gelatine, let stand until dissolved, then add the chocolate (after grating), and the rest of the milk; make very sweet. Cook carefully, as you would a boiled custard; if scorched 'tis spoiled; after it is thoroughly cooked, pour into a mould to harden and cool. For sauce, or dressing, use sweetened milk, or cream flavored with vanilla.

MRS. ROYAL MACK.

FLOATING ISLAND.

Four eggs, whites and yolks beaten separately, four heaping tablespoonfuls of powdered sugar, two teaspoonfuls almond or vanilla, one-half cup of currant jelly, one pint of milk. Make a custard of the yolks, sugar and milk, pouring the milk gradually when boiling hot, on the yolks and sugar. Flavor and pour in a glass dish. Put the beaten whites on top and dot with jelly.

MRS. BEERS.

DESSERTS.

One quart of cold boiled custard flavored with orange, one pint of whipped cream, sweetened, and flavored with vanilla. Mix and turn over one and one-half pints of oranges and bananas in equal parts, cut into small blocks; serve very cold.

Make one quart of ordinary corn starch blanc-mange, thin enough to eat without sauce. Omit the yolks, and add the beaten whites when partly cool. Stir in one-half pound of fresh chocolate creams until it colors in streaks. Serve cold.

☞ *Use SMITH'S COMMON SENSE Baking Powder and True-Fruit Flavoring Extracts. They are the best. See page 5.*

Peel bananas and suspend by running long slender wire through them. Boil to a syrup one-half pound of light brown sugar, one-fourth cake of chocolate, one-half cup of sweet milk, and butter the size of an egg. When this will hair, remove from the stove, and place in pan of hot water so that it will not cool too fast. Into it dip the bananas repeatedly until coated thickly with the caramel.

MRS. DESMOND.

CREAM CORN STARCH PUDDING.

Heat one pint of milk with one-half cup of sugar; when boiling, stir in four even tablespoonfuls of corn starch and boil until smooth. Remove from the fire and add three beaten whites, whipping them thoroughly into the pudding. Flavor with vanilla, and pour into a quart bowl which has been dipped in cold water. When very cold serve with a custard made of the yolks.

DANDY PUDDING.

Make a custard with one quart of milk, two tablespoonfuls of corn starch, one-half cupful of sugar, and the yolks of four eggs, adding the yolks last, just before removing from the fire. Flavor, pour into baking dish, cover with the whites beaten stiff and one tablespoonful of sugar. Put in the oven to brown. Serve icy cold.

MRS. MAKEHAM.

COFFEE SPONGE.

Add two cupfuls of sugar to one scant quart of strong coffee, boil, add one-half box of gelatine, soaked for two hours in one cupful of water. Remove from the stove as soon as the gelatine melts; stand in a cold place. When it begins to thicken, but before it is stiff, add the beaten whites of four eggs; stand the jelly in a pan of ice water, and beat all together fifteen minutes. Turn into a mold to harden. When ready to serve, stand the mould an instant in boiling water, invert, and the sponge will slip out easily. Serve with cream and sugar, or with whipped cream poured around it.

MRS. SERVOSS.

☞ Use *SMITH'S COMMON SENSE* Baking Powder and True-Fruit Flavoring Extracts. They are the best. *See page 5.*

PEACH SPONGE.

Beat a pint of fresh peaches to a smooth cream with an egg beater (the Keystone is best). Let three cupfuls of water and one of sugar boil for five minutes, add the peaches and boil five minutes longer. Then add one-half box of gelatine, which has been soaked for two hours in one-half cupful of water; as soon as the gelatine dissolves, remove from the fire and cool in a pan of ice water. When the jelly begins to thicken, but before it sets hard, add the stiffly beaten whites of three or four eggs, beat until thoroughly blended, standing the bowl meanwhile in ice water. When so thick that it will just pour, put in a mould or bowl and stand away to harden. When ready to serve, turn the mould over in a glass dish, wrap around it a cloth wet with boiling water for an instant, and then slip out the sponge. Serve with whipped or plain cream and sugar.

Sponges of many flavors are easily made, and in summer especially, are delicious. For all kinds, use a half box of gelatine for a quart of sponge, and vary the number of eggs to suit convenience.

For lemon or orange sponge, use the grated rind and juice of two to the pint of sponge. The yolks of the eggs may also be used, cooking them with the syrup and lemon.

A delicious sponge is made with one lemon, one pint of water, and one-quarter of a pound of candied cherries beaten in with the whites. Serve with boiled custard.

Make apricot the same as peach sponge. If canned fruit is used, drain and use the juice instead of water.

Use a quart of fresh strawberries or blackberries to a pint of syrup, rubbing the berries through a sieve after mashing them.

If the sponge gets too hard, before adding the whites, to beat well, soften it by standing in a pan of hot water.

SNOW PUDDING.

To one pint of boiling water and two cupfuls of sugar add the juice of three lemons, and one-half box of gelatine which has soaked for an hour in cold water. Strain this and cool. When cold and beginning to thicken, add the beaten whites of three or

---

Use SMITH'S COMMON SENSE Baking Powder and True-Fruit Flavoring Extracts. They are the best. See page 5.

four eggs and beat until snowy white. When thick enough so as to just pour, turn into the mould and set away to harden. This is the same as lemon sponge. To be served with a custard made of the yolks of the eggs. MRS. MAKEHAM.

CHARLOTTE RUSSE.

Whip one quart of sweetened and flavored rich cream to a froth and set on the ice. Dissolve one-third box of gelatine, soaked in a little water, in three-fourths of a cup of boiling milk. When very cold, add this to the whipped cream, and pour all into a glass dish lined with lady fingers or sponge cake. Set away to harden. MRS. ALVARADO STEVENS.

APPLE TAPIOCA.

Soak one teacupful of tapioca in cold water for one hour, drain, add to it one quart of boiling water, and boil in double kettle until transparent. Sweeten moderately and add six medium sized apples pared and quartered. Bake thirty minutes. Serve very cold.

For cherry, apricot or peach tapioca, soak the tapioca over night, simmer with one pint of water until clear, sweeten, add the stewed fruit as desired, and pour into the dish in which it is to be served. Serve very cold with sugar and cream.

COLD BERRY PUDDING.

Heat one pint of canned huckleberries, sweeten. Line the bottom of a quart bowl with buttered stale bread, add a layer of the boiling hot berries, then bread, and so on until the bowl is full. Press down with a weight. When cold, turn out of bowl, and serve with hot foamy sauce. Dried raspberries are good used this way. MRS. W. P. BIGELOW.

WEST END DESSERT.

Slice thin in a glass bowl four bananas, cover thickly with sugar, pour in the juice of two lemons, and stand two hours on the ice. MRS. ALDRICH.

☞ Use *SMITH'S COMMON SENSE Baking Powder and True-Fruit Flavoring Extracts. They are the best. See page 5.*

ICE CREAMS.

DIRECTIONS FOR FREEZING.

Pound the ice fine in a coarse bag and use coarse salt. Allow ten pounds of ice and two quarts of salt to a three-quart freezer. Have the first layer ice, three inches, then salt one inch, and so on to the top. After freezing the cream, take out the dasher, stir down, cover, and cork the hole in the cover; pour off the water, repack, and let it stand two hours before serving.

A covered tin pail set in a larger bucket makes a very fair freezer. Carefully remove the cover and stir occasionally, and between stirs, give the pail a slow whirling motion. In winter snow may be used in place of ice.

PLAIN VANILLA.

Heat one pint of cream in a double kettle, and when scalding hot, add one-half pound of sugar, and boil five minutes. When cold, add this boiled cream to one pint of cream, or if a plainer ice cream is desired, to one pint of milk. Flavor with vanilla and freeze. Boiling half the cream gives the peculiar velvety smoothness of the Philadelphia ice creams—it is not necessary but makes the most delicious creams.

MRS. W. A. MONTGOMERY.

PEACH OR APRICOT CREAM.

Beat one quart of fruit (if canned, without the juice), to a pulp with an egg beater. Mix three cups of good cream and two of milk; boil half of this with three-fourths of a pound of sugar until clear, cool; add to the rest of the cream; freeze. When partially frozen, add the fruit.

BANANA CREAM.

To one quart of mingled cream and milk, and one-half pound of sugar prepared as directed in previous receipts, add, when partially frozen, six bananas beaten to a pulp. Will serve nine.

☞ Use *SMITH'S COMMON SENSE Baking Powder and True-Fruit Flavoring Extracts. They are the best. See page 5.*

COFFEE CREAM.

Boil four tablespoonfuls of Mocha coffee in one pint of cream, and one-half pound of sugar; strain, cool, add another pint of cream; freeze. Will serve six.

FROZEN STRAWBERRIES.

Mash one quart of strawberries, then add one pound of sugar moistened with the juice of one lemon. Stir until the sugar is melted. Freeze.

FROZEN PEACHES.

One quart of water and three cupfuls of water boiled; one quart of peaches mashed. Freeze.

FROZEN BANANAS.

Boil one pint of water and two cupfuls of sugar; cool; add one dozen bananas beaten to a pulp and the juice of an orange. When nearly frozen, add a pint of whipped cream.

CURRANT WATER ICE.

One pint of red currant juice added to a cold syrup made of one pound of sugar and one pint of water; freeze. It will take much longer than ice cream to freeze. Delicious.

MISS MARY HALL.

LEMON WATER ICE.

The juice and grated rind of four lemons and one orange, add to a boiling syrup made of one quart of water and four large cups of sugar. Strain and freeze.

PICKLES AND CATSUPS.

CUCUMBER PICKLE.

Take cucumbers, wash and cover them with boiling hot water. Let them stand one day and wipe them dry. Measure the water to see how much vinegar to use. To one gallon of vinegar take one tablespoon of powdered alum, one teacup of salt, two tablespoons of mixed spices. Heat vinegar together with alum, salt and

---

Use SMITH'S COMMON SENSE Baking Powder and True-Fruit Flavoring Extracts. They are the best. See page 5.

spices, and pour over pickles ; let stand until next morning. Do this until vinegar has been boiled and poured over three times. Then slice a piece of horse radish over top, and wash grape leaves and cover over last thing.

This receipt can be depended upon; it makes hard green pickles that keep for years without any scum getting over the top.

Mrs. W. S. Kachler.

PICKLES.

To every hundred cucumbers, one pint of barrel salt ; pour boiling over them and let them stand over night. In the morning, wipe them dry with a towel ; then pour hot vinegar, spiced to suit the taste, over them.

Mrs. Servoss.

OIL PICKLES.

One hundred small cucumbers and one quart of onions sliced, and put in layers with coarse salt; stand aside all night under a heavy weight. Drain and pour over them enough cold vinegar, in which a tablespoonful of powdered alum has been dissolved, to cover them; stand six hours; drain. Mix together one-half pound of dry mustard, one-half cup of celery seed, one teaspoonful of black pepper, one pint of olive oil, and last two quarts of strong vinegar. Pour this mixture on the cucumbers and onions packed in glass jars ; fasten the tops and the pickles will be ready to use in two weeks. M.

RIPE CUCUMBER PICKLES.

Pare and scrape out the inside, put in a weak brine twenty-four hours. To a quart of strong vinegar add three pounds of sugar, and spice to taste ; into this boiling syrup put a few slices of the cucumber at a time ; boil until they look clear. When all are cooked, pour the syrup over them and put away in glass jars.

Watermelon rind may be pickled the same way.

GREEN TOMATO PICKLE.

Take medium sized tomatoes, slice thick ; cook in a weak brine till a fork will pierce them easily. Drain through a col-

☞ *Use SMITH'S COMMON SENSE Baking Powder and True-Fruit Flavoring Extracts. They are the best. See page 5.*

ander thoroughly, and put into vinegar for three or four days or a week. Drain off from this vinegar; then take equal parts of sugar and fresh vinegar; put in the fruit and heat to a boil. Put spices in a muslin bag and boil with the tomatoes; turn bag into your pickles with the rest. One teaspoonful cloves, one tablespoon cinnamon, one tablespoon mace, one tablespoon allspice.

Miss Susie E. Barrett.

SWEET TOMATO PICKLE.

One peck of tomatoes sliced, one teacup of salt, soak over night. Take two quarts of water and one quart of vinegar and put the tomatoes in and boil fifteen minutes. Throw this liquor away and then take two quarts of vinegar (reduced if very strong), and two pounds of brown sugar, one-half pound of white mustard seed, one tablespoonful of allspice, one of cloves, two of cinnamon, one of ginger. Put the tomatoes in this and boil until tender, about fifteen or twenty minutes.

Mrs. W. S. Kachler.

CHOPPED PICKLE.

One peck of green tomatoes, two quarts of onions, four peppers chopped; cook in salt water and then in weak vinegar until tender. Take five cups of fresh vinegar, two pounds of sugar, two tablespoons each of mustard, cinnamon, cloves, and one-third pound white mustard seed. Cook together two hours.

Ora B. Fry.

CHILI SAUCE.

One peck ripe tomatoes, six onions, four red peppers, one-half teacup salt, one and one-half cups sugar, three cups of vinegar. Chop onions and peppers very fine; boil the whole together two hours.

Mrs. Morrison.

PICKLED ONIONS.

Buy the small button onions, remove loose skin, stand in weak brine over night. Boil them until just beginning to be tender in weak vinegar, drain and put in glass jars. Cover them with strong hot vinegar, and seal.

☞ *Use SMITH'S COMMON SENSE Baking Powder and True-Fruit Flavoring Extracts. They are the best. See page 5.*

MIXED PICKLES.

Two dozen large cucumbers, two dozen green tomatoes, four large onions, two cauliflowers, two quarts small onions, two quarts cucumbers, two quarts beans.

Slice the large cucumbers, etc., and put each in separate dishes and soak over night in weak brine; then strain and cook till tender in weak vinegar, after which drain and put into crock or jar intended for the pickle.

Then make a paste as follows : two gallons vinegar, two cups flour, one pound mustard, two pounds brown sugar, one-half ounce celery seed, one-half ounce turmeric, one ounce cinnamon, one ounce cloves. Stir smooth with cold vinegar. Have the rest of the vinegar boiling, and add paste to it, stirring till the thickness of cream, then pour while hot over the pickles.

MRS. PEARCE.

PICKLED PEACHES OR PEARS.

Choose firm fruit not *very* ripe, gently rub off the down, place in layers in a stone jar and pour over them enough *boiling* vinegar to cover them ; let stand over night, drain. Make for each seven pounds of fruit, a syrup of three pounds of sugar, one pint of vinegar, and one tablespoonful of cinnamon. Stick two cloves into each peach, put them a few at a time into the syrup and cook slowly until clear. Skim out the peaches and place carefully in glass jars, cover with the syrup and seal. It is better to make these pickles a few at a time, as they loose their shape if crowded in the kettle. The vinegar in which they were soaked over night, may we used for several lots of pickles, one after the other. Pears may be pickled the same way, but do not need to stand over night.

M.

CHOW CHOW.

One pint each of tiny cucumbers, onions and string beans, one head of cauliflower ; cook together the onions, string beans and cauliflower until tender, but not soft; stand the cucumbers in strong brine over night. To two quarts and a half of vinegar, add, when boiling, a paste made of one-fourth pound of English mustard, one-fourth ounce of turmeric, one tablespoonful of

---

☞ Use *SMITH'S COMMON SENSE Baking Powder and True-Fruit Flavoring Extracts. They are the best. See page 5*

white mustard seed, one-half cup of sugar, and one cup of olive oil ; stir constantly until it thickens, then pour over the fruit which has been mixed and packed in glass jars.

SPICED GOOSEBERRIES.

Five quarts of fruit, three pounds of brown sugar, one pint of vinegar, a tablespoonful each of cloves and cinnamon ; boil all together until thick. Many add for this quantity two pounds of seeded and chopped raisins.

Mrs. A. S. Montgomery.

SPICED CURRANTS.

Five pounds of currants, four of sugar, one-half pint of vinegar, four tablespoonfuls of cinnamon, two of cloves. Boil three hours.

Ora B. Fry.

SPICED PLUMS.

Six pounds of damson plums, three of sugar, one pint of vinegar, cloves, allspice, cinnamon, each two teaspoonfuls. Boil about three hours. Very good with roast turkey.

Mrs. Sturgiss.

SPICED BLACKBERRIES.

Into a boiling syrup made of one pint of vinegar and two and one-half pounds of sugar, spiced to taste, put five quarts of ripe blackberries, and scald for about ten minutes.

TOMATO CATSUP.

One peck of ripe tomatoes, two heaping tablespoonfuls of salt, one of black pepper, two of mustard, one-half tablespoonful each of cloves, allspice, cinnamon, one-fourth teaspoonful cayenne, one pint of vinegar, two large onions. Boil together four hours.

Mrs. Brox.

GRAPE CATSUP.

Five pints of grapes cooked until soft and then put through a colander ; add two pounds of sugar, one pint of vinegar, six tablespoonfuls of mixed spice, and one-half teaspoon of cayenne. Boil until rather thick ; bottle.

Miss Satterlee.

☞ *Use SMITH'S COMMON SENSE Baking Powder and True-Fruit Flavoring Extracts. They are the best. See page 5.*

APPLE BUTTER.

To one peck of apples measured after being peeled and quartered, allow four pounds of brown sugar, and two quarts of water, and one cup of vinegar. Cook until smooth and thick. When nearly done, add spices to suit the taste. Stir constantly to avoid burning. Put up in jars like marmalade.

F.

JELLIES.

LEMON JELLY.

One box of gelatine, put in one pint of cold water, let it stand one hour, then add one pint of boiling water, one large lemon, one cup of white sugar, then strain. Make the day before using.

Mrs. A. Elwood.

ORANGE JELLY.

One-half box of gelatine dissolved in one cup of cold water, one large cup of sugar, juice of two oranges and a little of the grated peel, one lemon, juice and peel, one-half pint of *boiling* water. Strain through a bag into a mould and set aside to cool.

Mrs. C. S. Wheeler.

COFFEE JELLY.

One half box of gelatine softened in one-half pint of cold water; then add one-half pint of strong *boiling* hot coffee, sweetened with one-half cup of sugar. Add enough boiling water to make one and one-half pints of liquid. Strain into a mould to harden. Serve very cold with cream and sugar, or whipped cream.

Mrs. Wheeler.

LEMON FRUIT JELLY.

Make a rich lemon jelly with one box gelatine, three lemons, juice and grated rind, and one pound of sugar. Add the sugar and lemons to one quart of boiling water, and when all are boiling, pour over the gelatine which has soaked several hours in one

☞ *Use SMITH'S COMMON SENSE Baking Powder and True-Fruit Flavoring Extracts. They are the best. See page 5.*

pint of water. Put a layer of this jelly in the bottom of three one-quart moulds and let it harden. Then place on the first mould a layer of sliced bananas, in the second of English walnut, in the third of Malaga grapes. Pour over the fruit in each mould enough of the jelly to cover, and let this harden. Repeat this until the jelly is used up. Have the jelly poured over the fruit cold and a little thick, but not hard. Should it grow too thick, warm it a little by standing in hot water. In summer the moulds will need to be set in ice to harden each layer. Turn the three moulds out, side by side, into a large platter, pour whipped cream around them, and serve.

M.

CURRANT JELLY.

Select currants when they first ripen—they will not jelly well if dead ripe. Wash them and remove leaves, but do not stem. Mash thoroughly in a stone jar and then scald in a porcelain kettle. Pour the scalded currants into a flannel jelly bag, and hang the bag where it will drip into a stone jar over night; *do not squeeze at all.*

In the morning measure the juice, and bring it to a boil in porcelain kettle ; let it boil ten minutes before adding the sugar (which should be thoroughly heated in the oven), measure for measure. Boil rapidly after adding the sugar, skim carefully, and after five minutes, try it in a cold saucer to see if it will jelly; if not, boil a very little longer. Dip glasses in hot water, fill them and stand aside to cool. After two days, cover the tops of the jelly with writing paper dipped in alcohol, and then cover the whole with heavy paper, or the regular glass top. A second quality of the jelly, good to use for cakes, may be made by squeezing the pulp remaining in the bag after it has dripped all night. If a very fine color is desired, heat the juice two quarts at a time.

MRS. W. A. MONTGOMERY.

CRANBERRY JELLY.

Boil one quart of cranberries in one cupful of water until soft; mash, let them drain through a flannel rag. Return the juice to the fire and boil five minutes, add one pound of sugar and boil until it jellies, about five minutes.

☞ *Use SMITH'S COMMON SENSE Baking Powder and True-Fruit Flavoring Extracts. They are the best. See page 5.*

GREEN GRAPE JELLY.

Cook the grapes after stemming until soft. Pour into jelly bag, and drain all night. To three quarts of this juice, add a pint of cranberry juice strained. When boiling, add hot sugar measure for measure ; boil until it jellies. This jelly is much cheaper than the currant jelly and is almost as good.

JELLIED CURRANTS.

Put one pound of stemmed fruit into a granite kettle, and over it pour one pound of sugar. Bring to a boil carefully, so it does not burn ; boil twenty minutes and pour into jelly glasses.

MRS. BRADY.

BEVERAGES.

VIENNA COFFEE.

Add the stiff beaten white of an egg to one pint of cream, put in the cups with the sugar and pour over the hot strong coffee. The yolk of the egg can be used to settle the coffee. Whipped cream may be used instead of the white of an egg.

CHOCOLATE.

Scrape four squares Baker's chocolate, add six tablespoons of sugar and four of hot water ; stir over the fire until smooth and glossy ; add gradually to one quart of boiling milk. Beat it vigorously with an egg beater, and serve with whipped cream in each cupful.

BOUILLON.

Have four pounds of lean beef chopped fine ; pour over it two quarts of cold water, and simmer five hours in a closely covered granite kettle. Remove from the fire, strain, and when cool, add the beaten white of an egg. Put on again and boil until clear, skimming as fast as the scum rises. Season ; serve in little cups.

☞ *Use SMITH'S COMMON SENSE Baking Powder and True-Fruit Flavoring Extracts. They are the best. See page 5.*

RASPBERRY VINEGAR.

Pour one pint of cider vinegar over three pints of red raspberries and let stand twenty-four hours. Strain and add a pound of white sugar to every pint of juice; boil half an hour; bottle when cold. This makes a delicious drink in summer if diluted and sweetened.

Mrs. Hiram Doty.

GRAPE JUICE OR UNFERMENTED WINE.

To three quarts of grapes add one quart of water; boil one hour, strain. Add one pint of sugar to three pints of juice, boil half an hour, skim, and can boiling hot, like canned fruits. Use porcelain or granite ware in cooking, and glass jars for canning. Diluted one-third with ice water, this makes a delicious drink.

Deacon Hiram Doty.

OAT MEAL WATER.

First.—Put one cupful of uncooked oatmeal in a pitcher of ice water, stir several times, and let it settle. A very healthful drink for warm weather.

Second.—Boil one-half cupful of oatmeal in two quarts of water several hours until creamy and smooth. When cold, add a spoonful to a glass of ice water.

ESSENCE OF MEAT.

(VALUABLE IN ILLNESS.)

Take two pounds fillet of beef, remove all fat and skin, and cut the meat into small pieces; put into a wide-mouthed jar or bottle with salt and pepper. Tie down with a bladder, and set in a saucepan of water to boil for five hours, when the whole essence of meat will be extracted and look like oil. A teaspoonful to be taken at a time—equal to one mutton chop.

Mrs. T. Harwood Pattison.

BUTTERMILK POP.

Boil one quart of buttermilk in a double kettle, add one small tablespoon of corn starch moistened with a little milk. Drink when cold, with or without sugar. Good for dyspepsia.

☞ *Use SMITH'S COMMON SENSE Baking Powder and True-Fruit Flavoring Extracts. They are the best. See page 5.*

MISCELLANEOUS.

TO REMOVE STAINS.

For fruit stains in linen, pour boiling water through the linen.
For coffee stains in linen, pour boiling water through the linen.
For cream stains, soak in cold water; hot water will set the stain.
For ink stain, rub on lemon and salt and place in the sun.
For mildew, rub on the article while wet a paste made of soap and chalk, equal parts, and place in the sun.
For iron rust, rub the spot with sulphuret of potash, then bathe in lemon juice and wash in water.

TO BRIGHTEN TINWARE.

Rub on it a little common baking soda, well moistened. This will keep it beautifully bright and sweet.

CHINA CEMENT.

Get pure gum arabic, and make a thick solution with water. Stir in enough plaster of Paris to make a white paste. Apply to the broken edges and stick them together. In three days the dish may be used, with no fear of it breaking again in the same place.

TO CLARIFY FAT.

Mrs. Rorer gives the following directions : Melt the drippings to be clarified, and strain into a clean pan; add to every three pounds of this fat a pint of boiling water and a quarter-teaspoonful of baking soda. Boil until the water has all evaporated. Skim and strain, and it is ready to use. Fat that has been used for croquettes or fried cakes, may be clarified again and again.

WASHING FLUID.

One pound-can Babbitt's potash, one-half ounce sal amonia, one-half ounce salts of tartar, dissolved in two gallons of water. Use one-fourth cup of this fluid to a tub of water. In preparing the fluid, dissolve the potash in hot water, and use a stone jar in dissolving the sal amonia and salts.   MRS. ROSA NODYNE.

☞ *Use SMITH'S COMMON SENSE Baking Powder and True-Fruit Flavoring Extracts. They are the best. See page 5.*

TO OPEN A CLOGGED WATER PIPE.

Dissolve a pound of Babbitt's potash in boiling water, pour into the sink or bowl, and it will eat out the obstruction in the pipes. A few hours after, wash out the pipe thoroughly with boiling water. This simple device will often save sending for a plumber.

TO KEEP WOOLEN CLOTHING AND FURS.

Heavy woolens and furs should be put away early, before the moth miller is abroad. Hang out the furs where the sun shines hot, and thoroughly brush and comb them, and let the warmth of the sun penetrate every part. Put the muff in its box, and paste a strip of paper perfectly smooth and tight where the cover joins the box. See that the box is whole, and there is no danger of moth. Larger fur garments may be sealed tightly in paper bags, made of heavy manilla paper, and be perfectly safe.

Winter overcoats should be thoroughly brushed, *sunned*, and hung on a wire holder; then all inserted in a paper bag made the length and width of the coat. Paste the top of the bag *tightly*, allowing the wire loop only to project; have no tiny hole anywhere. Hang the overcoat by a hook in the top of the closet and it will come out fresh and unwrinkled. If garments are properly sunned and sealed tightly, no camphor or pepper is needed.

If winter flannels and woolen pieces are wrapped securely in newspaper—several wrappings, then tied securely,—leaving no break, they will be safe. Leave no woolen pieces exposed to breed mooths, but have all laid away in tight paper bags or wrappings, and you will have no trouble with moths.

TO CURE HAMS.

To every twenty pounds of ham, take one pint of salt, one ounce of saltpetre, one pint of molasses; dissolve all in just enough water to cover the ham. Repack every week, and in four weeks they will be salt enough to smoke.

DEACON DOTY.

TO CLEAN PAINT.

Save tea leaves from the table, steep them in a tin basin—do not boil—half an hour; strain and use on the paint.

☞ *Use SMITH'S COMMON SENSE Baking Powder ana True-Fruit Flavoring Extracts. They are the best. See page* 5.

www.ingramcontent.com/pod-product-compliance
Lightning Source LLC
Chambersburg PA
CBHW022143090426
42742CB00010B/1364